"Tell me what you eat and I will tell you what you are."

— Anthelme Brillat-Savarin

Physiologie du Gout, ou Medetations de Gastronomie Transcendante

"I cannot remember the books I've read any more than the meals I have eaten;
even so, they have made me."

— Ralph Waldo Emerson

What Do You Eat?

Sourcing & Cooking Pure Foods

Amy Thurber

CRICKET
WORKS
PRESS

Cricket Works Press
South Dartmouth, MA 02748

Distributed to the trade by CricketWorksPress.com

Library of Congress Control Number: TXu 2-220-500
Library of Congress Cataloging-in-Publication Data

Names: Thurber, Amy, author.
Title: What DO You Eat?/ by Amy Thurber ; Cover, and interior photography and illustrations by Amy Thurber.
Description: First edition. | South Dartmouth : Cricket Works Press, [2022]
Identifiers: LCCN TXu 2-220-500 | ISBN 978-1-7345019-1-9 (paperback)
Subjects: Cooking | Recipes | Food Allergies | Paleo | Specific Carbohydrate Diet | Local Foods | Pure Cooking
Printed in the United States of America on 50# white paper

CricketWorksPress.com

First edition 1 2 3 4 5 6 7 8 9

Book design by Amy Thurber

Text set in Cochin. Titles set in Brillon and Adine Kernberg Script.

CRICKET
WORKS
PRESS

TABLE OF CONTENTS

How To Use *this Cookbook*

Everyone has their own dietary needs. Most recipes in this book lend themsleves to variations, so when possible I have included suggestions for substitutions and options. This allows you to tailor them to your own individual needs. Here is more information about the dietary key used in the recipe sidebar.

SCD
The Specific Carbohydrate Diet encourages healthy eating while avoiding ingredients that can feed bad bacteria in your gut. For a full list of "Legal and Illegal" foods see the website: **https://www.scdrecipe.com/legal-illegal-list/listing/all**. Where possible I've included substitutions for non-SCD compliant ingredients in the margin under Options.

Paleo
Paleo guidelines encourage fresh local produce, grass-fed meats, and discourage processed foods, starches, sugars and nightshades (such as tomatoes, potatoes, peppers and eggplant).

GF = Gluten-Free & Grain-Free
All the recipes in this cookbook are Gluten-Free as well as Grain-Free.

Nut-Free
Nuts are not called for in the ingredient listings, but when a recipe calls for either flaxmeal or sunflower meal, you may substitute either almond flour or other nut meal. This is especially important if you are on the SCD diet. Flax and sunflower seeds are not recommended while following the SCD diet.

DF option = Dairy-Free option
If you are dairy intollerant, or trying to avoid dairy to reduce inflammation, you may substitute the butter, milk, or half-and-half with non-dairy products.

Vegetarian option
Many of the recipes are vegetarian, even though they are not labeled as such. Some recipes also offer alternatives to animal products. Remember, just because a recipe is paleo doesn't mean it can't also be vegetarian or vegan.

Low Nickel
It is nearly impossible to avoid nickel altogether, however I have made note of recipes which contain foods low in nickel. Remember that metal cooking equipment can contribute to nickel exposure. See the Appendix for more information about a nickel allergy.

1   tsp = teaspoon   Tbs = tablespoon   unswt. = unsweetened

Navigating the Recipes

Sidebar gives additional information like the number of servings, dietary key, Options and Notes.

The Recipe Title is followed by a tidbit about the recipe. Options for alternate ingredients are noted by an ⁕ with more details in the margin.

Sidebar Key allows you to find recipes that fit your needs at a glance. See categories in more detail on the opposite page.

Makes 4 to 6 servings

CURRIED BUTTERNUT SQUASH SOUP

I crave these warm, satisfying flavors come autumn.

1 small or 1/2 large butternut squash peeled and cubed
1 1/2 Tbs butter or substitute⁕   2 apples peeled and diced
1 large onion chopped   1 - 2 Tbs curry powder⁕⁕
1 stalk celery chopped   1 cup cider
2 large carrots chopped   3 cups chicken broth⁕
salt and pepper to taste   2 Tbs cilantro leaves
5 Tbs coconut milk

1. Preheat oven to 400° F. If using a whole butternut squash, wash and place in large glass or ceramic baking dish. Pierce skin on top with a knife. Bake squash for 30 minutes. Let cool, and cut in half, remove seeds, skin and cut into cubes. If using pre-peeled or cut squash, cube and proceed.

2. Place butter in a deep soup pot over medium heat. Add onion and saute until transparent. Add celery, carrots, apples, squash, and curry powder to taste. Saute until lightly browned and fragrant. Add cider and broth and bring to a simmer. Cook until all ingredients are very soft.

4. Using an immersion blender, or food processor, blend until smooth. Serve warm, garnished with 1 Tbs coconut milk and cilantro leaves.

SCD option
Paleo
GF
Nut-Free
DF option
Vegetarian option⁕

Options:
Vegetarian Option:
⁕ Substitute olive oil or plant based butter for butter, and vegetable broth or more cider for the chicken broth.

SCD option:
⁕⁕ Omit curry powder

DF option:
Substitute dairy-free butter for the butter.

Note:
Years ago, I had an unfortunate finger injury while cutting up a winter squash. I've found a short roasting, adds flavor, while also making it safer to peel and chop.

Options gives information on recipe ingredients and substitutions.

Notes gives more information on cooking techniques and other helpful tips.

Page Number
See the index for listings by recipe title and diet types or ingredients.

49

2

INTRODUCTION
to Pure Foods

When someone asks me to describe my diet, the inevitable next question is, "So...What DO you Eat?" It's not hard to rattle off a list of my staples, and they sound pretty much like everyone's shopping list:

• Fruits   • Vegetables   • Meats & Fish   • Seeds

It's the omissions that have them flummoxed:

NO: Sugars   NO: Grains   NO: Nuts   NO: Dairy   NO: Starchy Vegetables

I remember the day my son and I started changing our diet. He had been diagnosed with Crohn's disease, and I had chronic hives. A friend had told me about the Specific Carbohydrate Diet, and I had just taken Kendall Conrad's book, *Eat Well, Feel Well* out of the library. Our plates were an artistic spread of apple and cucumber slices, brie, and smoked trout. That lunch began our journey to better health. Six years later, I am grateful for taking that first step, and happy to share with you what I have learned.

Over the past few years I have eliminated from my diet anything that causes inflammation, or an allergic reaction. Allergies and food intolerances are on the rise, and learning to prepare foods that those with gut issues and allergies are able to eat can be fun and enjoyable. When you feel good on your diet, it's all the incentive you need to keep it up. Eating this way also has significant health benefits for many people, whether you have food intolerances or not.

One of the biggest challenges I had when I began this dietary journey was sourcing foods that were free of unwanted ingredients, sugars, and starches. I found the fewer ingredients, the easier it was to ensure I had control over what I was putting in my body. When I refer to "Pure Foods" I mean sourcing single or minimal ingredient foods that satisfy the body's needs *3* without including foods your body reacts to. These recipes use "Pure Foods" to create meals that eliminateallergens and inflammatory ingredients.

Specific Carbohydrate Diet (SCD)

Developed by Elaine Gotteshall, the Specific Carbohydrate Diet works by allowing beneficial bacteria to flourish while starving out the bad bacteria. When you eliminate the foods that the bad bacteria feed on, your beneficial bacteria thrive. This creates a healthy intestinal track and immune system. This diet has been found to be helpful for those struggling with Crohn's disease, irritable bowel syndrome (IBS), and other digestive and inflammatory issues. Even people without these issues experience health benefits.

Paleo Diet

The paleo diet has been very popular and for good reason. It makes you feel strong and healthy, gives you plenty of energy and can help you lose weight. Sourcing food is an important part of the paleo diet. Organically grown produce and ethically raised livestock who graze in pastures are much healthier for us and the planet.

Gluten-Free

Those who are gluten intolerant are aware of the increase in sugars and starches in many gluten-free baked goods and processed foods. By eliminating grains and sugars, we can still uphold the gluten free criteria while delivering something even more nutritious.

Dairy-Free

This was a tough one for me to give up. For years I resisted the good advice from my doctors about eliminating dairy. However once I did, I realized how long I had been reacting to it, causing me inflammation and hives. There are some good alternatives to butter and milk, but nut-free cheeses are hard to find. I did find a delicious sunflower based cheese at Plant City in Providence, RI.

Other Allergies

Over the years I have had allergies to chocolate, dairy, gluten, cashews, mushrooms, spices, apples, artificial fragrances, citrus, nuts, and nickle. I've been able to tolerate reintroducing some of these foods. Some continue to cause skin reactions, joint pain and inflammation. Allergy testing is key to unraveling your own body's needs.

Nickle in Cooking Equipment

I have reacted to metal on and off since a small child. Jewelry would give me a rash, and wearing earrings, watch bands, and necklaces was out of the question. After finding I had a severe nickle allergy through skin patch testing, my first step was changing my pans to ceramic lined cookware, and glass bakeware. These are easy to find and relatively inexpensive. When I use a cookie sheet, I always line it with parchment paper. I love tea, but my metal tea kettle had to go. I began boiling water in a borosilicate glass kettle, and steeping my herbal teas in a good old-fashioned ceramic tea pot.

4

Next came tools. Wooden spoons, rubber spatulas, and glass or ceramic bowls were already in my kitchen. I changed to ceramic knives, plastic or rubber whisks, and wooden or plastic flatware. Believe it or not, when I go out to eat, everything has a metallic taste now. I was never aware of this before, but with this "clean" cooking, food really does taste better. Even if you are not reacting to nickle, practicing this method of cooking has its rewards in the clean flavor of the foods.

Nickle in Foods

Most foods contain trace amounts of nickel, so it is impossible to completely eliminate it from your diet. However, there are certain plants that tend to "hold" nickle. (See the appendix for more information about nickel.) Keep in mind that plants absorb nutrients from the soil they are grown in, so depending on where they are grown, their nickle content can be variable.

When considering nickel content in foods I like to focus on the cumulative rather than the individual ingredients I consume throughout the day. Picture your day as a cup. You are adding nickel exposure at each meal. When you've reached the brim of the cup, it starts over flowing. This is the point where your body reacts. Everyone's cup is a different size. Try not to be "afraid" of foods that contain nickel. But do be aware of how much you can tolerate. Many foods that contain moderate amounts of nickel are also very beneficial in other ways. So learn your boundaries, and remember to enjoy what you are eating.

Another source of nickel exposure can be from skin products, dish and laundry soap, and household surfaces. Coconut and nut oils are commonly found in skin and soap products. These can cause a reaction for some people with an allergy to nickel. Read the labels on items you use regularly, and if necessary look for alternatives. (See the appendix for suggestions.)

Histamine in Foods

According to Wikipedia: "Histamine is an organic nitrogenous compound involved in local immune responses, as well as regulating physiological function in the gut and acting as a neurotransmitter for the brain, spinal cord, and uterus. Histamine is involved in the inflammatory response and has a central role as a mediator of itching."

While histamine intolerance (HIT) is rare, it's good to be aware of a few facts. There are foods high in histamine, and those that trigger it. A Web search can help you identify these foods. Histamine levels increase as foods age. To reduce histamine intake, avoid prepared or frozen foods and eat plenty of fresh meats and produce.

Consult your doctor before starting a new diet. I've developed and included recipes that exclude foods that I am allergic to. Feel free to experiment with the ingredients to see what works for you. – AT

Tips for Tackling Allergies

Once you've identified what you are reacting to, you can eliminate it from your diet and find substitutes. I try to avoid falling into the habit of pretending I'm eating something I'm not. For instance, if you want a cheeseburger, but can't have the bun or the cheese, then try adding new toppings to a beef patty. Serve it on lettuce, add homemade mayonnaise or ketchup and sugar-free bacon, caramelized onions, sliced avocado, sprouts or fresh tomato, and you have something worthy on its own.

Where possible, I've included ingredient substitutions in the recipe sidebar to help those with various allergic conditions. All recipes are free from processed sugars, nuts, and grains. When substituting ingredients in the recipes, just keep in mind the health benefits of eliminating these ingredients.

Eating Out & On the Go

Ordering at restaurants, cafés, and take-out is easy if you stick to simple dishes. If they are using good ingredients, even plain food is delicious. Baked or broiled fish, and steamed or sauted vegetables are generally free of hidden ingredients. If ordering salad, I ask for simple oil and vinegar for dressing. When in doubt ask about the ingredients.

Sometimes I'll order a sandwich and slip the good stuff out of the bread. If a dish comes with an unexpected ingredient, I just eat around it. I always ask for any sauce to be served on the side. When I explain that I have multiple allergies, the staff are usually happy to oblige. I don't rely on gluten-free foods on the menu, as most contain grains, starches and sugars.

When packing food for travel, I try to keep to non-perishable items. Good choices are sunflower apricot bars, muffins, rosemary flax crackers, dried fruits, jerky and toasted sunflower seeds. If I can keep things cool, I'll add pasta salad, quiche, hummus, and hard boiled eggs. A hearty salad with protein can keep me going for hours.

SOURCING Pure Foods

The Provenance of Foods:

In Parma, Italy the pigs are fed whey, a by-product of the famous Parmigiano Reggiano cheese. These pigs are revered for the fine quality prosciutto they produce. While living in Italy during college, I remember experiencing the reverence with which the Italian farmers regarded their products. The way in which the food was produced, the history of the land, and the variety of the plants were very important to them. While enjoying a delicious bowl of homemade pasta, I committed to memory the steps our hostess outlined for preparing the pasta. Something as simple as how to boil the water had meaning and importance.

It is no wonder the term, "you are what you eat" rings true. We are, after all, at the end of a long chain of lives and events that produce what we eat. We can't help but be impacted by the food chain. But so few of us are aware of this.

There have been studies showing the health benefits of grass-fed beef, as well as the detrimental affects of beef raised on genetically modified corn. It's bad for the cows, as well as bad for us. In the race to produce more food, and transport it great distances while increasing it's shelf life, we have sacrificed our health, as well as that of the planet and the plants and animals we raise for food. To get the same nutritional content of an apple produced 100 years ago, you would need to eat 15 modern day grocery store apples. What has happened in the past century? Degradation of our soils, and breeding programs that focus on storage and size over taste and nutrition.

Derek Christianson of Brix Bounty Farm, in South Dartmouth, MA, has been an advocate for restoring soil health. He has taught workshops on how to increase the "brix" in produce by feeding the soil. Brix is a measure of natural sugars and nutrients in plants. A strawberry with a high brix will taste sweeter, last longer, and is more resistant to diseases. Lessons such as this help to reinforce the importance of sourcing high quality, locally grown food.

The enthusiasm for heirloom vegetables and animal breeds is another nod to the benefits of historic agriculture. After the Irish potato famine, the importance of cultivating a wide diversity of plant strains was recognized. Having access to more variety in the gene pools of the foods we rely on provides protection against large-scale crop failures. Older

8

9

breeds of vegetables have a higher nutritional content, and heirloom breeds are delicious. The only drawback to heirloom vegetables is that they don't always store well. For this reason, you may only be able to access them through local farms or by growing them yourself.

Just imagine the difference between a peach that was picked green, and shipped hundreds of miles in a refrigerated truck to get to your grocery store, versus one you just picked, ripe off the tree. Go ahead, take a bite. Can you taste where they came from?

So next time you wander through your garden, be sure to nibble on the green beans, pop some ripe cherry tomatoes into your mouth, and chomp on some spinach. It's what we are meant to do.

Online Foraging

It can be a challenge to source prepared foods for people with allergies. The good news is, if you stick to fresh produce, local meats and fish, and buy simple staples in bulk, you will have a good healthy selection of foods to choose from. When it comes to pantry staples, sauces, and canned foods, I include a selection of those I use in Pantry of Pure Foods which follows. Explore what is available in your area, but when in doubt, read the labels.

Growing Your Own

There is nothing more gratifying or delicious than growing your own food. Rent a plot at your local community garden, or if you have a sunny space, replace some grass with and home garden. Growing vegetables, permaculture (fruit trees, berry bushes, asparagus, and rhubarb), and raising hens for eggs are some of the best ways to ensure a healthy food supply.

Local Farms

There are many new ways to get your food from local farms. Now more than ever, it's important to support local growers.

Community Supported Agriculture (CSAs) allow the farmers to project how much food to grow, while giving them funds early in the season when they need them the most. You benefit by getting a weekly supply of quality produce at a discount.

Online ordering is becoming a popular way to access foods from local farms. We get weekly orders of meats, produce, handmade soaps, candles, and farm-produced goods from several of our local farms. Check with your local farm associations for suggestions.

Farm stands and farmers markets are another way to access local foods. My husband Frederick loves the social scene at the Westport farmers market. After filling me in on all the local news, he proudly presents his treasures such as tiny cartons of quail eggs and bunches of spring onions held like a bouquet of roses.

Foraging & Fishing

If you have wild areas near by, look for wild edibles. Always double check your identification before consuming wild plants. *Stalking the Wild Asparagus*, by Euell Gibbons and *Wild Plants I Have Known and Eaten* by Russ Cohen are great resources for foraging. Beginners foragers should never forage for wild mushrooms without an experienced guide. I only buy mushrooms from reputable local sources, and never collect them from the wild.

Fishing can be a fun way to acquire fresh, healthy protein. Check with your local fish and wildlife organization for the regulations and open seasons.

Food Cooperatives

If you know someone who is part of a food cooperative, ask about becoming a member. If not, you can search for companies in your area that support food cooperatives. Some of these companies are the same ones that supply health food stores. Many times they sell bulk foods like 25 lb. bags of navy beans, 5 lbs of dried apricots, cherries or mangos. Getting staples this way is usually less expensive, and allows you to access simple organic ingredients while minimizing shipping, packaging, and avoiding the stores. Coop families are a great support network as well. See appendix resources (p. 153).

Making Your Own

I've had very good luck making my own sunflower meal, mayonnaise, ketchup, salad dressing, marinades and pesto. If you have a food processor, a bowl and a whisk, you can too. See the section on Basics & Extras (p. 133) for recipes and instructions.

Checking Ingredients

When purchasing items that appear to be whole foods, it's always good to check the ingredients. Even dried fruits can have added sugars. One unlikely source of sugars is bacon, sausage, and cured meat. In some cases the sugars are altered during the curing process, and the resulting acids help preserve the meat. When in doubt, there are some sugar-free bacon brands available.

Know Your Beans - Ingredients That Cause Inflammation

Just because a bean is oval and white doesn't mean it's a haricot (navy) bean. This may seem picky but white kidney beans, cannellini, garbanzo beans, and many other dried beans have enough complex carbohydrates to cause intestinal problems. However, navy beans and lentils are usually well tolerated once you've gotten your inflammation stabilized. Black beans can also be fine. All beans must be soaked and rinsed to remove the indigestible complex sugar called oligosaccharides. Lentils and lentil pasta are great substitutes for grain pastas and have lots of protein. Just be sure to soak and rinse the dried lentils before cooking, and rinse the cooked pasta before serving.

11

Potatoes are very high in complex carbohydrates, however I have found I can tolerate sweet potatoes once in a while. Other root vegetables that are usually well tolerated are celery root and rutabaga, but taro and turnips can cause intestinal problems.

Seeds and grains are another case in point. Even ancient grains such as quinoa, amaranth, spelt and rye are high in complex carbohydrates. In particular corn and rice are inflammatory due to their high starch and sugar content. Unfortunately, these two grains are the most common flour substitutes in gluten-free baked goods. Seeds on the other hand are usually well tolerated and are full of protein and healthy oils.

Sweet Stuff

Honey and fruit are sweet, but their sweetness is derived from a simple carbohydrate that doesn't usually cause bad gut bacteria to flourish. Complex sugars such as cane sugar, brown sugar, molasses, high fructose corn sugar, and even maple syrup can cause inflammation and intestinal problems by feeding bad bacteria in the gut.

When in doubt, check to see if an ingredient is Specific Carbohydrate Diet approved: http://www.breakingtheviciouscycle.info/legal/listing

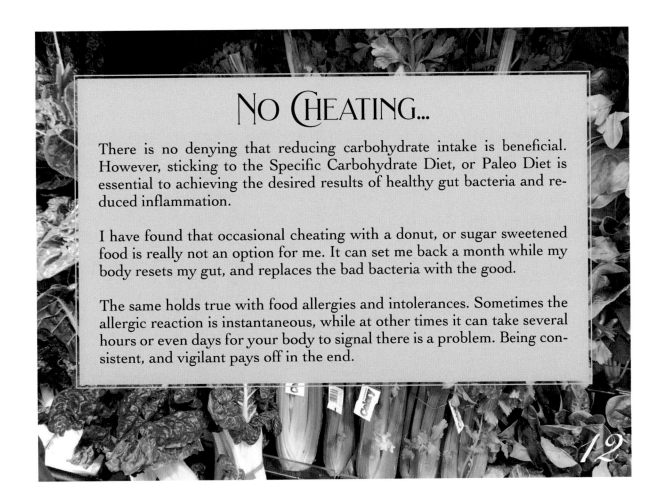

NO CHEATING...

There is no denying that reducing carbohydrate intake is beneficial. However, sticking to the Specific Carbohydrate Diet, or Paleo Diet is essential to achieving the desired results of healthy gut bacteria and reduced inflammation.

I have found that occasional cheating with a donut, or sugar sweetened food is really not an option for me. It can set me back a month while my body resets my gut, and replaces the bad bacteria with the good.

The same holds true with food allergies and intolerances. Sometimes the allergic reaction is instantaneous, while at other times it can take several hours or even days for your body to signal there is a problem. Being consistent, and vigilant pays off in the end.

PANTRY
of Pure Foods

Pantry items are staples referred to frequently in the recipe section. These brands are only suggestions, so please feel free to source your own pantry items. Just be sure to read the ingredient listings carefully. *Note: I'm not being compensated by any of these companies, nor is this considered advertising. I'm merely sharing products that I have found helpful.*

SWEETENERS

Avoiding refined sugars goes a long way in reducing inflammation. Sweeteners like honey, fruit-sweetened jams and dried fruits are healthy substitutes. Date sugar is okay in small quantities if you're not experiencing gut symptoms. While maple syrup is a natural sugar, it should be avoided if you are following the Specific Carbohydrate Diet because it is a disaccharide, which can feed harmful gut bacteria.

13

Baking: Grains, Nuts, Seeds, & Flours

If you have a gluten intolerance, there are many flour mixes to choose from. If your goal is to reduce gut symptoms and inflammation, going one step further to grain-free is very helpful.

Those who tolerate nuts, can enjoy almond, cashew, hazelnut, and pecan flours. If nuts are a no-no, try coconut flour. It works well in many recipes. Use coconut sparingly however, if you have a nickel allergy. When using shredded coconut, be sure it is unsweetened.

With the exception of the Specific Carbohydrate Diet, seed meals are also an available substitute for grains.

Flax meal has the added benefit of omega-3 fatty acids and healthy fiber. It also acts as a binder in baked goods, much the way gluten would. Chia, poppy, and sesame seed add variety and texture.

Sunflower seeds can be made into flour or butter, toasted and added to pesto and scattered atop salads. Use caution when introducing seeds if you're experiencing gut symptoms.

If you are using chocolate in your baked goods look for chocolate sweetened with stevia. For those who avoid chocolate, carob is a wonderful caffeine-free alternative to cocoa.

Here are some tricks to cooking dried beans to minimize inflammatory effects. Beans, Lentils and Peas are high in nickel, so avoid them if you have a nickel allergy.

Cooking Dried Beans, Lentils & Split Peas

The night before, place dry navy beans, lentils, peas, split peas, adzuki beans, or lima beans in a large pot, and cover with 4 to 6 cups of water. Let sit until morning. Drain and refill with fresh water. Place over medium high heat, and bring to a boil. Allow to simmer for 1 hour or until beans are soft. Drain, rinse, and put aside. Alternatively, you can use canned navy beans. Rinse again before using. This process eliminates lignin, an insoluble fiber which causes digestive issues. Do not soak dried beans for more than 10 hours.

There are some delicious dried bean pastas available. Good choices for reducing inflammation include lentil and dried green pea pasta. Check ingredient listings carefully as many bean pastas include rice or other starches. If you're following the Specific Carbohydrate Diet (SCD), avoid black bean, garbanzo bean, and soy bean pastas.

I've included a recipe for making your own green pea pasta. This can be used fresh if you can't find pre-made green pea pasta. It's best to use sprouted green pea flour.

When cooking pasta made with dried beans, the texture is best if slightly undercooked. Rinse with fresh water before adding sauces and toppings. Then reheat if needed.

15

Avoiding Added Sugars & Starches

Keep an eye on ingredient listings. Some tomato products, plus marinated and pickled vegetables, may contain sugars and starches. I like to find foods with the fewest ingredients. They tend to be good quality products, and delicious to boot!

What to avoid: sugar, sucrose, high-fructose corn syrup, wheat, rice, rice starch, potato starch, carrageenan, guar gum, vegetable gum, tapioca starch (not SCD compliant), and cornstarch. For a full list of SCD-compliant ingredients visit: **https://www.scdrecipe.com/legal-illegal-list/listing/all**

OTHER STAPLES

Some table salt brands contain dextrose which should be avoided. Sea salt contains lots of added minerals that are beneficial. But be sure you're getting some iodine. Sea salt with kelp, such as the herbed sea salt above, is a natural source of iodine.

SunButter is a good choice for those with nut allergies. Tuna in glass jars is a plus for nickel allergies. Grass-fed beef gelatin is an excellent thickener for desserts and contributes healthy collagens to your diet.

Most prepared condiments contain sugar. It's not hard to make your own mayonnaise, ketchup and pesto. Look for mustards that contain only mustard seed and vinegar.

DAIRY

If you are lactose or dairy intolerant, there are many options for substitutions. Most of these, however, are nut or oat-based. Some also have starches as thickeners. For those avoiding nuts, coconut-based dairy is a good option. If you are following the SCD, look for coconut milk that doesn't contain carrageenan.

Vegetarian butters act very much like real butter. Try to avoid hydrogenated oils for heart health. Other baking staples are lard and duck fat both of which have been used for centuries. For the past 50 years they were shunned, but recently they are being recognized as healthy and delicious additions to baked goods, and cooking. Animal fats also stay stable at higher temperatures and are excellent for frying.

If following a Low Nickel Diet, avoid coconut and nut-based milk products.

Substitutions: The recipes in this book offer many substitutions. However, if you attempt to replace the coconut flour with grain flour, the consistency of the end product may be very different. Feel free to experiment when substitutions are noted.

USEFUL *Kitchen Tools*

If you are new to cooking, or would like more information about some of the references to cooking tools listed in the recipes, here is a guide.

Whisks and Egg Beaters:
These add volume and air to liquids and help blend batters thorougly. If you have a nickel allergy look for silicone-covered whisks.

Stick Blender:
Immersion blenders are handy tools for creating creamy soups and silky smoothies.

Pastry Blender or Cutter:
I use this tool to blend fats into dry ingredients. It also does a good job creating a crumbly topping for fruit crisps and streusels.

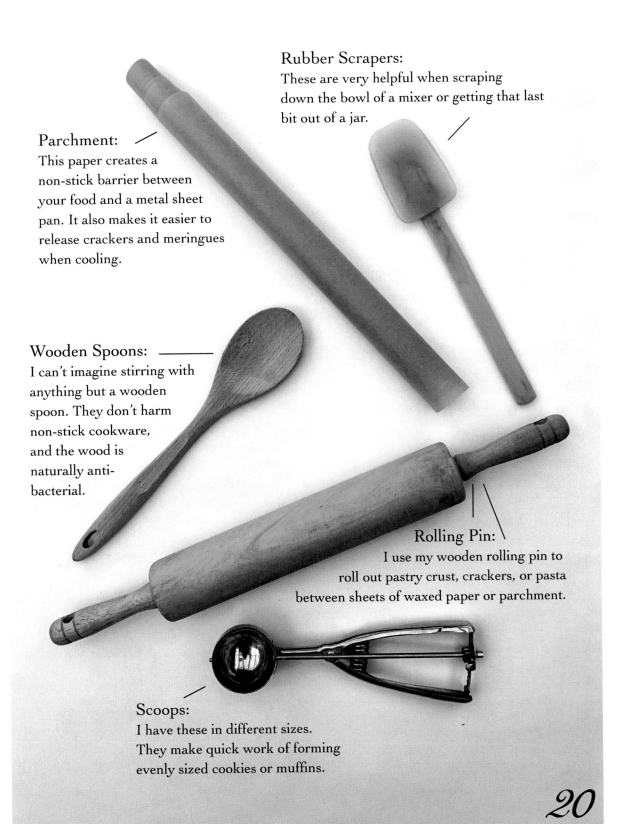

Parchment:
This paper creates a non-stick barrier between your food and a metal sheet pan. It also makes it easier to release crackers and meringues when cooling.

Rubber Scrapers:
These are very helpful when scraping down the bowl of a mixer or getting that last bit out of a jar.

Wooden Spoons:
I can't imagine stirring with anything but a wooden spoon. They don't harm non-stick cookware, and the wood is naturally anti-bacterial.

Rolling Pin:
I use my wooden rolling pin to roll out pastry crust, crackers, or pasta between sheets of waxed paper or parchment.

Scoops:
I have these in different sizes. They make quick work of forming evenly sized cookies or muffins.

20

Breakfast: a Clean Start

Have you ever been told, "Breakfast is the most important meal of the day"?

Well, it's true! A dietitian friend once told me that the first thing you put in your mouth after fasting dictates what your body will crave for the remainder of the day. So if you begin your day with a sugary carbohydrate, your body will quickly use up the energy and continue to crave more. Alternatively, if you begin your day with a protein-rich meal, your body will be satisfied, and when hunger strikes again, it will crave more good meals.

The act of breaking your fast, or breakfast, is the practice of moving your metabolism from resting and storing energy in the form of fats, into ramping up cellular activity and using energy. If you fail to give your body this signal by skipping breakfast, you will remain in resting mode, and your energy level and cognitive function will suffer.

While a typical American breakfast involves sugary cereal, milk, and coffee, or juice, our day usually begins with bacon, eggs, tea, and a grain-free baked good. You don't have time to cook, you say? Well, I usually bake once every few days, and not always in the morning, and cooking the bacon and eggs takes about as long as steeping my tea.

On weekends we sometime enjoy grain-free pancakes, or crepes, but almost always accompany them with bacon, sausage, or proscuitto. When camping, we have scrambled or hard boiled eggs, porridge, muffins, and jerky to start our day. There's no doubt we need the fuel on our long hikes. So why should any other day be different?

Once you get into this routine, you'll find your energy level and calm core from a happy stomach will be reward enough to keep it up.

22

Breakfasts

GOOD OL' FRIED EGGS

SCD
Paleo
GF
Nut-Free
DF
Low Nickel

Options:
Top eggs with home-made mayonnaise, pesto, roasted red pepper, tomato, fresh minced herbs, or micro greens.

If omitting the bacon step, heat 1/2 Tbs olive oil in pan before frying eggs.

*Look for sugar free bacon.

One of our favorite breakfasts is fried eggs. When I began this diet, I remember thinking I couldn't eat a fried egg without toast. Ha! They are exquisite on their own or dressed up with toppings. And the cooking process makes it a wonderful morning ritual.

4 to 6 eggs (2-3 per person)   1 small red onion sliced thin
2 to 4 slices of bacon*   salt and pepper to taste

1. Heat a 10' to 12" ceramic skillet over medium-high heat. Cook the bacon until browned and crisp. Remove bacon to plates, and leave grease in the pan.

2. Lower heat to medium. Add sliced onion to pan, and saute until well browned. Remove onion to plates.

3. Lower the heat to medium low. Break eggs into the grease and cook gently, flipping when still slightly transparent on top. When cooked to your liking, remove to plates and top with onions and salt and pepper to taste.

SCD option
Paleo option
GF
Nut-Free
DF option

Options:
**Can substitute:
dried dates, apricots,
cranberries, cherries
or raisins soaked in
1 Tbls of fruit juice,
rum or water,
OR fresh strawber-
ries or cranberries.

SCD option:
Substitute almond
flour for sunflower
meal and omit flax-
meal.

Paleo, SCD & DF:
Use dairy-free butter.

Note:
*If using unsalted
butter, increase salt
to 1/2 tsp.

Sunflower meal is
very high in nickel.
Eat it sparingly if you
have a nickel allergy.

BLUEBERRY SCONES

This recipe is so versatile you can make many substitutions.

1/3 cup flax meal
1 cup sunflower meal
1/2 cup coconut flour
2 Tbs date sugar (optional)
1/4 tsp sea salt
milk, coconut milk, or water as needed

1/2 tsp baking soda
1 tsp nutmeg
1/3 cup honey
1/2 cup butter or substitute*
1/2 to 3/4 cup blueberries**

1. Preheat oven to 350° F. Blend together dry ingredients in a medium-sized mixing bowl.

2. Add honey and butter or butter substitute, and blend with a pastry blender. (Can also be made in a food processor up to adding blueberries.) Add enough milk or water to form a stiff dough. Gently mix in the blueberries.

3. Form into 6 mounds on parchment lined baking sheet, and flatten to 1/2" with wet fingers. Sprinkle with additional date sugar if desired.

4. Bake at 350° F for 20 to 25 minutes.

Apple Fritters

SCD option
Paleo option
GF
Nut-Free
DF option

3 Tbs butter or substitute*
2 large eggs
2 Tbs golden flax meal
2 Tbs coconut flour
2 apples, peeled, cored and grated (approximately 1 1/4 cups)**

1 Tbs honey plus more for topping
1/2 tsp ground nutmeg
1/2 tsp ground cinnamon
1/4 tsp sea salt

1. In a medium-sized bowl, whisk eggs. Add flax meal, coconut flour, honey, salt, and spices. Blend, then add grated apples and mix together.

2. Heat a 12" skillet over medium-high heat. Melt 2 Tbs butter, and place 3 mounds of apple batter in skillet. Flatten to 1/2" thick with a spatula.

3. Fry apple fritters until nicely browned, then gently flip and brown the other side. When done, move to a plate and keep warm.

4. Melt remaining 1 Tbs butter in skillet, and repeat the process with the remaining batter.

5. Serve with a bit of butter and a drizzle of honey.

Options:

SCD option:
Substitute almond flour for flax meal.

Paleo, SCD & DF:
Use dairy-free butter.

Note:
*If using unsalted butter, increase salt to 1 tsp.

** I like using firm apples like cortland or macoun.

Hold-the-Cheese Omelet

So many things pair beautifully with eggs. Have fun experimenting and making substitutions. I doubt you'll ever miss the cheese.

2 Tbs olive oil or fat
5 to 6 eggs
1 small onion
1/2 colored pepper, diced

1 cup broccoli crowns, chopped
2 Tbs fresh chives, snipped
salt and pepper

SCD
Paleo
GF
Nut-Free
DF

Options:
• Asparagus, red onions and fresh dill

• Roasted tomatoes, prosciutto, and thyme.

• Spinach, roasted tomatoes. and scallions

• Zucchini, basil pesto, tomatoes, and onions

• Sweet potato, shallots, and arugula

1. Whisk together the eggs in a mixing bowl. Put aside.

2. Heat 1 Tbs of the olive oil or fat in a 12" skillet over medium high heat. Add onions and peppers, and cook until onions are transparent. Add broccoli, and 1 Tbs of water. Cover and cook until broccoli is bright green, approximately 2 minutes. Remove cover, and let any moisture evaporate. Leave vegetables in the pan.

3. Reduce heat to medium low. Add remaining 1 Tbs of olive oil. Swirl around to coat the bottom of the pan. Add the beaten eggs and 1 Tbs of chives to the vegetables. While cooking, slide a spatula underneath to allow the liquid egg to coat the bottom of the pan. When almost set, fold omelet in half and press. When set to your liking, cut in half and place on plates. Sprinkle with 1 Tbs of chives.

Rum-Raisin Cinnamon Bread

This bread is light, fluffy and satisfying.

SCD option
Paleo option
GF
Nut-Free
DF option

1/2 cup raisins soaked in 1 Tbs rum, cider, or water
4 Tbs butter or substitute, softened*
1/3 cup honey
6 eggs
3/4 cup coconut flour
1/4 cup flax meal
3/4 tsp baking soda
1/4 tsp sea salt

Swirl Mixture
2 Tbs butter or substitute, softened
2 Tbs honey
1 Tbs cinnamon

Options:
Try substituting
dried cranberries for
the raisins.
If you can tolerate cit-
rus, grated orange peel
is a nice addition to the
batter.

SCD option:
Substitute almond
flour for flax meal. Use
water or cider in place
of rum.

Paleo, SCD & DF:
Use dairy-free butter.

Note:
*If using unsalted
butter, increase salt to
1/2 tsp.

1. Preheat oven to 350° F. Soak raisins in rum, and put aside. Mix together swirl ingredients and put aside. Grease an 8"x 8" pan and put aside.

2. Cream together butter and honey. Add eggs, coconut flour, and flax meal and blend until light and fluffy. Add baking soda, salt, and raisins along with their soaking liquid. Mix well.

3. Spread batter evenly in 8" x 8" pan. Drop swirl mixture all over batter, then swirl lightly into batter using a fork.

4. Bake for 30 minutes at 350° F, or until just set and lightly brown.

SCD option
Paleo
GF
Nut-Free
Spice-Free
DF option

Options:
*Experiment with different dried fruit. Some of my favorites are:
- dried cherries
- raisins & cinnamon
- dried apricots
- dried cranberries
- dried mango

I also like to add diced fresh banana or apple.

SCD option:
Substitute almond flour for flax meal.

DF option:
Substitute dairy-free butter for the butter and dairy-free milk for the milk.

Coconut, flaxseed and chia seed are very high in nickel. Eat them sparingly if you have a nickel allergy.

COCONUT PORRIDGE

I create a bulk dry mix of this breakfast staple, to keep in the fridge. That way it's easy to portion it out for a good stick-to-your-ribs breakfast. This has sustained us on long tramps in New Zealand.

Bulk Porridge Mix:
1 1/2 cups golden flax meal
3 cups unsweetened shredded coconut
1/4 cup chia seeds

Single Serving:
1/3 cup porridge mix (above)
2/3 cup milk or substitute, fruit juice or water
1/4 tsp salt
2 Tbs dried or 1/4 cup fresh fruit*
Butter or butter substitute and honey to taste for serving

Place ingredients in sauce pan and simmer, stirring until thick. Serve warm with dairy-free butter and honey.

30

MANGO MUFFINS

SCD option
Paleo option
GF
Nut-Free
Spice-Free
DF option

Options:
You can substitute
dried pineapple, apri-
cots, or pears for the
mango.

SCD option:
Substitute almond
flour for flax meal.

Paleo, SCD & DF:
Use dairy-free butter.

Note:
*If using unsalted
butter, increase salt
to 1/2 tsp.

The bright flavors and sunny color of these muffins make it a great way to start the day.

1/3 cup of butter or substitute⁕ | 1/4 tsp sea salt
1/4 cup honey | 1/2 tsp baking soda
1 Tbs date sugar (optional)
6 large eggs
5 pieces of dried mango re-hydrated in 1/2 cup boiling water to cover
1/2 cup coconut flour
1/4 cup golden flax meal

1. Preheat oven to 350° F. Line 12 muffin cups with paper liners, or use silicone muffin pans. Chop cooled mango into 1/4" pieces, and reserve 1 Tbs of soaking liquid.

2. Place butter, honey, and date sugar in mixer and combine. Add eggs and mix. Add flax meal, coconut flour, sea salt and baking powder. Beat on medium/high for one minute or until light and fluffy. Add mango and 1 Tbs of liquid and mix.

3. Scoop batter into muffin cups. Bake at 350° F for 20 to 25 minutes.

**SCD option
Paleo option
GF
Nut-Free
DF option**

Options:
**Substitute fresh
strawberries,
peaches, cherries, or
raspberries for the
blueberries.
If using frozen fruit
add while still frozen,
and increase cooking
time by 5 minutes.

SCD option:
Substitute almond
flour for flax meal
and omit date sugar.

Paleo, SCD & DF:
Use dairy-free butter.

Note:
*If using unsalted
butter, increase salt
to 1/2 tsp.

FRESH BLUEBERRY MUFFINS

This is a new version of a breakfast classic. The smell is irresistible when you take them out of the oven. It's sure to get everyone out of bed.

1/3 cup of butter or substitute*
1/3 cup honey
1 Tbs. date sugar *(optional)*
6 large eggs
1/2 cup coconut flour
1/4 cup golden flax meal

1/4 tsp sea salt
1/2 tsp baking soda
1/2 tsp nutmeg
1 cup blueberries**
(1 Tbs date sugar mixed
with 1/4 tsp nutmeg *optional*)

1. Preheat oven to 350° F. Line 12 muffin cups with paper liners, or use silicone muffin pans.

2. Place butter, honey, and date sugar in mixer or a large bowl, and combine. Add eggs and mix. Add flax meal, coconut flour, sea salt, nutmeg, and baking soda. Beat on medium/high for a minute or so till light and fluffy, then add the blueberries and mix gently.

3. Scoop batter into muffin cups, filling 3/4 full. Sprinkle the top with more date sugar mixed with nutmeg if you'd like. Bake on middle shelf of preheated 350° F oven for 20 to 25 minutes.

PUMPKIN SPICE MUFFINS

These are moist and full of Autumn flavors. I enjoy them with a bit of butter and pear fruit jam.

SCD option
Paleo
GF
Nut-Free
DF option

1/3 cup of butter or substitute * 1/4 tsp ground cloves
1/3 cup honey 1 tsp ground nutmeg
1 Tbs date sugar (optional) 1 tsp ground cinnamon
6 large eggs 1/2 tsp baking powder
2/3 cup pumpkin puree ** 1/4 tsp sea salt
1/2 cup coconut flour 1/4 cup golden flax meal
1/2 cup dried-fruit juice sweetened cranberries

1. Preheat oven to 350° F. Line 12 muffin cups with paper liners, or use silicone muffin pans.

2. Place butter, honey and date sugar in mixer or food processor, and mix until light and fluffy. Add eggs, and pumpkin puree and mix at medium speed until frothy.

3. Add dry ingredients and combine. Then stir in dried cranberries.

4. Scoop batter into muffin cups, filling 3/4 full. Sprinkle tops with additional date sugar if you'd like. Bake at 350° F for 20 to 25 minutes, or until puffed and just cooked through. Let cool slightly before serving.

Options:
**Substitute sweet potato puree for the pumpkin, and raisins for the dried cranberries.

SCD option:
Substitute almond flour for flax meal and omit date sugar.

Paleo, SCD & DF:
Use dairy-free butter.

Note:
*If using unsalted butter, increase salt to 1 tsp.

SCD option
Paleo option
GF
Nut-Free
DF option

Options:
SCD option: Substitute almond flour for flax meal.

Paleo, SCD & DF:
Use dairy-free butter.

Note:
*If using unsalted butter, increase salt to 1/2 tsp.

**To toast coconut, spread evenly on a rectangular baking dish. Place in preheated 350° F oven for 5 to 10 minutes. Watch it very closely so it doesn't burn. Remove when lightly browned.

BANANA DONUTS

Batter

2 ripe bananas, diced
1/2 cup coconut flour
1/4 cup golden flax meal
1/3 cup honey
6 large eggs
1/2 cup of butter or substitute, plus more for greasing pan.*

1/3 cup dried unsweetened coconut
1 Tbs date sugar (optional)
1/4 tsp sea salt
1/2 tsp baking soda
1/4 tsp ground cardamom

Frosting

1/3 cup butter or substitute softened
1 1/2 Tbs carob powder   2 1/2 Tbs honey

Garnish with 4 Tbs dried unsweetened coconut, toasted**

1. Preheat oven to 350° F. Generously butter the inside of 8 to 12 holes of a silicone donut pan. Place pan on sheet pan to keep them flat. Put aside.

2. Place bananas, flax meal and coconut flour in mixer and blend until banana is completely incorporated. Add eggs and mix well. Add butter, honey, and date sugar and mix until light and fluffy. Then mix in the dried coconut, sea salt, cardamom, and baking soda.

3. Scoop batter into donut cups. Bake at 350° F for 20 to 25 minutes or until just set. Allow to cool for 15 minutes before removing from pans. Place donuts on a cooling rack or plate.

4. Mix together frosting ingredients in a small bowl. Once the donuts have cooled, spread frosting on top, and sprinkle with toasted coconut. Serve immediately.

Scrambled Eggs with Herb Butter

SCD option
Paleo option
GF
Nut-Free
DF option
Low Nickel

Options:

You can also make these with plain butter, olive oil, or other fat.

Low Nickel:
Use dairy butter

Paleo, SCD & DF:
Use dairy-free herb butter.

The trick to moist scrambled eggs is to remove them from the pan while there is still some liquid egg. They will continue to cook for a few minutes even on your plate.

2 Tbs herb butter *(p. 138)*
6 large eggs

1. Preheat 10" or 12" skillet on medium-low heat.

2. In a bowl beat eggs until just frothy.

3. Melt 1 1/2 Tbs herb butter in pan, and immediately pour in eggs. Stir until barely set and still moist. Serve with 1/2 Tbs of remaining Herb Butter on top.

SCD option
Paleo option
GF
Nut-Free
Spice-Free
DF option

Options:
*Substitute: fresh strawberries, cherries or raspberries for the blueberries.

SCD option:
Substitute almond flour for flax meal.

Paleo, SCD & DF:
Use dairy-free butter.

Banana Pancakes with Blueberries

Bananas make these pancakes moist and sweet.

2 ripe bananas diced
2 Tbs flax meal
3 to 5 Tbs coconut flour
2 Tbs butter or substitute

1/4 tsp sea salt
4 large eggs
1/2 cup blueberries*

1. In a bowl, blend together banana and dry ingredients using a pastry blender, or food processor. Add eggs and mix well. The batter should be the consistency of pourable yogurt. If too thin, add more coconut flour 1 Tbs at a time. Let sit a few minutes before adding any additional coconut flour. Add blueberries and stir until just incorporated.

2. Preheat 12" skillet over medium-high heat. Melt fat and swirl to coat bottom. Drop 1/4 cup of batter into skillet, and flip when browned underneath. When both sides are browned, place on serving plate.

3. Serve with butter and honey, fruit jam, or date syrup.

PORK SAUSAGES

SCD
Paleo
GF
Nut-Free
DF
Low Nickel

Options:

❋ You can use this mixture in soup. I like forming it into balls, browning them in the soup pot, removing them, then adding them back into the soup at the end.

If you'd like to have some of these on hand for breakfast, roll into logs, and wrap individually in waxed paper, then freeze for future use. Thaw in the refrigerator the night before use.

Since many sausages contain sugars and starches, I've provided a recipe for home-made pork sausages. I don't have a sausage maker, but if you do you can put them in casings.

1 lb. ground pork
1 small onion minced
1 small garlic clove minced
2 - 3 dates pitted and minced
1/2 tsp smoked sea salt

1/2 tsp dried thyme
1/2 tsp dried marjoram
1/2 tsp dried sage
1/4 tsp ground pepper
1 Tbs olive oil

1. Place all ingredients except olive oil in a food processor. Pulse until just mixed. Refrigerate in an airtight container for future use, or form into 3/4" thick, sausage shaped logs or balls for soup.❋

2. Heat a skillet over medium high heat. Fry sausages for 10 to 15 minutes, turning frequently, until well browned and cooked through and no longer pink inside.

Apple Oven Pancake

Many cultures have a version of this delicious oven pancake.

Batter:
4 eggs
1/2 cup milk or substitute
1/4 tsp sea salt**
2 Tbs coconut flour

Apple Mixture:
2 medium apples cored, peeled and sliced thin*
4 Tbs butter or substitute, divided
2 tsp cinnamon
3 Tbs honey

1. Preheat oven to 400° F. In a bowl, whisk together eggs, milk, coconut flour and salt. Mix well and put aside.

2. Preheat 12" non-stick, oven-proof skillet over medium high heat. Melt 2 Tbs of butter and add apples, honey and cinnamon. Saute until apples are browned, the liquid bubbles and is sticky and caramelized. This should take 5 to 10 minutes depending on the type of apple.

3. Leave apple mixture in the pan, but push aside to the edges. Melt remaining 2 Tbs of butter, and pour in the batter. Stir slightly to incorporate apple mixture.

4. Place skillet in preheated oven, and bake 15 to 20 minutes, or until puffed and brown on edges.

5. Divide into servings while in the pan using a rubber spatula. Remove to a serving platter or individual plates and serve warm.

SCD option
Paleo option
GF
Nut-Free
DF option

Options:
* Substitute: fresh pears or peaches for the apples

Paleo, SCD & DF: Use dairy-free butter and milk.

Note:
**If using unsalted butter, increase salt to 1/2 tsp.

38

Apple Streusel Cake

Paleo option
GF
Nut-Free
DF option

Note:

*If using unsalted butter, increase salt in the cake batter to 1/2 tsp.

Options:

Paleo & DF:
Use dairy-free butter.

** You can substitute fresh peaches or pears for the apples. My favorite type of apple to use for this recipe is Macintosh.

Notes:

Sunflower meal is very high in nickel. Eat it sparingly if you have a nickel allergy.

Streusel Topping - Mix together and refrigerate until needed.

1/2 cup sunflower meal	1/2 tsp cinnamon
1/4 cup flax meal	1/4 cup butter or substitute
1/4 cup coconut flour	1/4 tsp salt
2 Tbs date sugar	1 Tbs honey

Cinnamon Butter - Mix together, and put aside until needed.

2 Tbs honey	2 tsp cinnamon
2 Tbs butter or substitute, softened	

Cake Batter -

1/4 cup flax meal	1/2 tsp baking soda
6 eggs	1/4 tsp salt
1/2 cup butter or substitute*	1/2 tsp each cinnamon & nutmeg
1/2 cup honey	1/8 tsp ground cloves
1/2 cup coconut flour	1 cup diced apples**
1/3 cup yogurt or substitute	

1. Preheat oven to 350° F. **Cake Batter-** mix flax meal and eggs in a large bowl or mixer, and let sit for 5 minutes. Add butter and honey and blend. Add remaining dry ingredients and mix.

2. Spread batter into an 8" x 8" baking pan. Distribute diced apple over top of the batter. Dot with cinnamon butter mixture. Crumble streusel topping evenly over the top. Bake for 25-30 minutes or until topping is golden brown, and cake is evenly puffed. Do not over cook.

SCD
Paleo
GF
Nut-Free
DF option

Options:
*SCD & Paleo:
Use dairy-free milk
and butter.

** You may also
use banana bread,
or muffins to make
French toast. I slice
the muffins in half
horizontally.

Notes:
Gluten-free baked
goods can fall apart
easily. Don't over
soak, or the bread
may be difficult to
handle. Thicker
slices make it easier
to remove from the
soaking liquid.

French Toast

If you have leftover baked goods, French toast makes a quick and delicious break-fast or brunch offering.

3 eggs
1/2 cup milk or substitute*
1 Tbs honey
6 to 8 slices rum-raisin cinnamon bread *(p. 29)* **

1/2 tsp cinnamon or nutmeg
1 Tbs date sugar
2 Tbs butter or substitute*

1. In a small deep bowl, whisk together eggs, milk, honey, date sugar, and cinna-mon. Mix well and place half the cinnamon bread in the batter to soak. Let soak for 1 to 2 minutes then turn over.

2. Preheat 12" non-stick, oven-proof skillet over medium high heat. Melt 1 Tbs of butter and add the first batch of soaked cinnamon bread. While these are cooking, soak the next batch of cinnamon bread.

3. Cook the bread on all sides until browned, and repeat with remaining bread, adding additional butter as needed.

4. Serve drizzled with honey.

Gardening, Farming, *& the Barter System*

My father's vegetable garden seemed vast to my young eyes. There were endless rows of peas, beans, peppers, carrots, parsnips, and squash. I would marvel at the way things evolved from soft brown earth to a solid green sea of foliage. He included some unusual plants such as kohlrabi and fennel, and beet greens for my grandmother. At the end of the season, he would bring armloads of produce to his pediatric office to distribute among the staff and patients. In exchange, he would receive gifts of homemade sun dried tomatoes, delectable homegrown fruit and baked goods.

I used to wonder, why the abundance? Why were so many gardeners producing more than they could use, and then eagerly giving the surplus away?.... Enter the voracious woodchuck, the devious deer, the greedy ground hog, the rambunctious rabbits, the pesky chipmunk and eager cat bird, not to mention the slugs, snails, white flies, aphids and cabbage moth caterpillars. Any seasoned gardener knows that you are bound to loose some of a crop to predators, insects and disease. If you diversify, plant in abundance, and protect from natural invaders, you're more likely to get some for yourself. And when luck is on your side, you share the bounty with fellow two-legged friends.

At the beginning of our relationship, my husband Frederick was a tenant on River Rock Farm. The 200-acre gentleman's farm raised black Angus and had a beautiful kitchen garden with many wild edibles. After one enjoyable bird watching adventure, we returned to Fred's little house to find Mrs. Schimd, the owner of River Rock, had left us an entire clam bake in the kitchen sink. We frequently found her gifts of asparagus, strawberries, and even frozen River Rock chickens on the door step. These were her way of saying thank you for his weekend work doing farm chores. But I suspect it was deeper than that. Frederick's nature writing and generosity in sharing his knowledge of the farm's wild inhabitants with her created a wonderful bond. Throughout his stay at River Rock Farm, he kept her updated on the wild side of the farm. His regular reports included coyote sightings, news of the neighborhood barn owl, the amphibian migrations, and the shrike that left it's prey on the barbed wire farm fence. In turn we helped with haying, feeding the cows, steers, pigs, hens, and a peacock. We participated in the seasonal cycles at the farm, and enjoyed cooking its delicious bounty.

Bartering has great value in the gardening and farming world. I inevitably start way too many tomato and squash seedlings for my garden beds. I trade these with garden friends for seedlings of plants I'd like to try, such as celery, chipolata onions, and

41

ramps. Sometimes a crop fails, and I am able to swap with a fellow gardener to fill in a garden row. When I still have more plants than I can find homes for, I donate them to our local community garden for their soup kitchen garden.

Frederick loves salt-water fishing. On his way back from the launch ramp he usually calls me to put out the bluefish alert. We trade bluefish for Eva's greens, and Round the Bend Farm's grass-fed meats. Our friend Bette will transform Frederick's blue fish into succulent smoked slabs, and return some of the bounty to us in payment.

When Frederick's collection of fragrant rhododendrons are blooming, we put out another invitation for garden tours. Friends and their friends come to sniff and admire these ephemeral beauties. In exchange they sometimes bring gifts. Yesterday we enjoyed asparagus from Dorian's garden, beef from Jordan Farm, and curried hubbard squash soup with onion flowers from chef Didi Emmons. All were fresh treats, prepared with thought and given with generosity. Bartering is a language of gratitude fluent among gardeners and farmers. It is a never ending cycle which enriches our lives.

42

Soups & Salads

SOUPS

SALADS

Pumpkin & White Bean Soup

SCD
Paleo
GF
Nut-Free
DF
Vegetarian

Options:

*If you're cooking this on the stove top, the smoked salt adds a lot of depth to the flavor of this soup. If you can't find smoked salt, you can substitute plain sea salt.

You may also use bone broth or chicken stock in place of the vegetable broth for non-vegetarians.

Notes:

Beans are very high in nickel. Eat them sparingly if you have a nickel allergy.

I like to cook this over an open fire, but the stove top is fine too.

1 Tbs olive oil or fat
1 large onion chopped
1 leek sliced (white part)
2 cloves of garlic minced
3 carrots chopped
2 stalks celery chopped
1 large cooking pumpkin (to make 5 cups diced pumpkin)

2-15 oz. cans of navy beans, rinsed
6 cups vegetable
smoked salt* and pepper to taste
3 sprigs of fresh thyme
2 sprigs of fresh rosemary
1 bay leaf

1. Preheat oven to 375° F. Place whole pumpkin in a glass or ceramic baking dish. Puncture the top in 3 places with the point of a knife. Bake for 20 to 30 minutes, or until pumpkin is slightly softened. Allow to cool.

2. When cool enough to touch, cut pumpkin in half, then scrape out and remove seeds. Using a vegetable peeler, remove skin. Dice the pumpkin into bite-sized pieces. Measure out 5 cups, and put aside for later.

3. In a large soup pot over medium high heat, add olive oil, onion, leek, and garlic. Cook until transparent. Add celery and carrots. Cook for 10 minutes until slightly browned.

4. Add pumpkin, navy beans, broth, smoked salt, pepper, and herbs. Raise heat to high. Bring to a boil, then reduce heat to medium. Cover and simmer for approximately 1 hour, stirring occasionally, until pumpkin is soft and broth has thickened. If soup becomes too thick, add water a little at a time. Taste to adjust seasonings.

SCD
Paleo
GF
Nut-Free
DF

SPLIT PEA SOUP

A big pot of this soup makes me feel that all is well with the world.

<u>Night Before</u>
Soak 2 cups of split peas in 6 cups of water.

<u>Soup</u>

1 Tbs olive oil or fat
1 large onion chopped
2 stalks celery chopped
1 bay leaf
2 cloves of garlic minced

6 slices of no-sugar bacon, diced
3 carrots chopped
smoked salt and pepper to taste
2 sprigs of fresh thyme
6 cups pork or chicken stock

1. Cook bacon in large soup pot. Remove from pot when brown and crisp, and reserve for garnish. Leave bacon fat in pot.

2. Add olive oil and onions to pot, and cook until transparent. Add celery, garlic, and carrots. Cook for 10 minutes or until slightly browned.

3. Drain split peas in strainer, rinse, and immediately add to soup pot.
(I've learned not to pause here, unless you want to be digging a solid split pea lump out of your colander.)

4. Add bay leaf, salt, pepper, fresh thyme, and stock to the pot. Cover and bring to a low boil. Stir and reduce heat to low. Simmer soup covered for 1 hour, stirring occasionally, until peas begin to dissolve into the broth. Add water if soup becomes too thick. Taste and correct seasonings.

5. Serve topped with reserved bacon and a drizzle of good quality olive oil.

Options:
This recipe is also excellent with left-over diced pork from a butt roast or ham in place of bacon. Proceed to step 2.

If you have the bone, try making the stock with it. The flavor and health benefits are worth the time.

Notes:
Split peas are very high in nickel. Eat them sparingly if you have a nickel allergy.

46

47

CARROT SOUP WITH TARRAGON

Tarragon has a distinctive savory licorice flavor. It pairs nicely with the sweetness of carrots. Be sure to use good quality carrots for this soup, and it will be memorable.

2 Tbs olive oil, plus more for garnish
1 large onion chopped
2 stalks celery chopped
4 cups carrots chopped (6 lg.)
2 small sprigs fresh tarragon
1 bay leaf
4 cups un-salted chicken stock
1/2 tsp sea salt
1/4 tsp pepper

1. Heat the oil in a large soup pot over medium-high heat. Saute the onions until transparent. Add celery and carrots and cook, stirring occasionally, for 10 minutes until slightly brown.

2. Add fresh tarragon (reserve a few leaves for garnish), bay leaf, salt, pepper, and stock. Bring to a low boil. Lower heat to medium low and cover. Simmer soup for 20 to 30 minutes, or until the carrots are very soft. Taste to correct seasonings.

3. Allow to cool slightly, then puree soup with stick blender, or food processor. You can blend bay leaf into soup, but if it's tough, remove bay leaf and discard before blending.

5. To serve, place the soup in bowls, top with reserved snipped tarragon leaves and a drizzle of good quality olive oil.

SCD
Paleo
GF
Nut-Free
DF
Low Nickel
Vegetarian option

Options:
If you don't have fresh tarragon, you can use 1 Tbs of dry tarragon.

You can also substitute fresh or dried chervil for the tarragon.

Vegetarian Option:
Use vegetable broth in place of chicken stock.

CURRIED BUTTERNUT SQUASH SOUP

SCD option
Paleo
GF
Nut-Free
DF option
**Vegetarian
option**⁎

Options:

Vegetarian Option:
⁎ Substitute vegetable broth or more cider for the chicken broth.

SCD option:
⁎⁎ Omit curry powder

DF option:
Substitute dairy-free butter for the butter.

Note:
Years ago, I had an unfortunate finger injury while cutting up a winter squash. I've found a short roasting, adds flavor, while also making it safer to peel and chop.

I crave these warm, satisfying flavors come autumn.

1 small or 1/2 large butternut squash peeled and cubed
1 1/2 Tbs olive oil
1 large onion chopped
1 stalk celery chopped
2 large carrots chopped
salt and pepper to taste
5 Tbs coconut milk
2 apples peeled and diced
1 - 2 Tbs curry powder⁎⁎
1 cup cider
3 cups chicken broth⁎
2 Tbs cilantro leaves

1. Preheat oven to 400° F. If using a whole butternut squash, wash and place in large glass or ceramic baking dish. Pierce skin on top with a knife. Bake squash for 30 minutes. Let cool, and cut in half, remove seeds, skin and cut into cubes. If using pre-peeled or cut squash, cube and proceed.

2. Place butter in a deep soup pot over medium heat. Add onion and saute until transparent. Add celery, carrots, apples, squash, and curry powder to taste. Saute until lightly browned and fragrant. Add cider and broth and bring to a simmer. Cook until all ingredients are very soft.

4. Using an immersion blender, or food processor, blend until smooth. Serve warm, garnished with 1 Tbs coconut milk and cilantro leaves.

MINESTRONE

Comfort food, as well as a great way to use garden surplus.

1 large onion chopped
1 1/2 Tbs olive oil
1-2 cloves garlic sliced
2 carrots diced
2 stalks celery chopped
1/2 colored pepper chopped
1 zucchini squash diced
1 sprig each parsley, oregano, and thyme

1/2 cup green beans in 1" pieces
4 plum tomatoes chopped*
3-4 cups broth
1 can of navy beans rinsed**
1 cup lentil or pea elbow pasta
1 bay leaf
salt and pepper to taste

1. Place butter in a deep soup pot over medium heat. Add onion and saute until transparent. Add garlic, carrots, celery, zucchini and pepper. Saute until lightly browned and fragrant.

2. Add green beans, tomatoes, broth, and navy beans and bring to a boil. Reduce to a simmer, add herbs and cook for approximately 15 to 20 minutes or until vegetables are just soft.

3. Add pasta and cook another 10 minutes. Serve warm.

Makes 4 to 6 servings

SCD
Paleo
GF
Nut-Free
DF option

Options:

Add diced sweet Italian sausage.

*Or substitute one 16 oz. can of diced tomato for fresh. If using fresh tomatoes peel and remove seeds before adding to reduce inflammation.

** If you can't find canned navy beans, you can substitue dried navy beans. The night before making the soup, place 1 cup of dried navy beans in a pot with 4 cups of water and bring to a boil. Drain and cover with fresh water. Soak them in the soup pot over night. Test for softness and drain and rinse before using.

50

Fish Chowder

Any firm white fish is good in this chowder. The celery root replaces the potato used in a classic chowder.

SCD
Paleo
GF
Nut-Free
DF option
Low Nickel

Options:
*Cod, sea bass, haddock, or halibut are good choices

5 slices of no-sugar bacon chopped
1 Tbs olive oil or fat
1 large onion chopped
2 stalks celery chopped
1 celery root peeled and diced
1 1b. white fish fillets cubed*

3 cups fish or chicken stock
2 sprigs fresh thyme
1 bay leaf
salt and pepper to taste
fresh parsley for garnish

1. Heat a large soup pot on medium-high heat. Add chopped bacon and cook, stirring frequently, until browned and crisp. Remove to a plate, leaving the fat in the pot.

2. Add additional oil or fat and onions to the pot and saute on medium heat until transparent. Add celery and diced celery root and continue to saute for another 5 minutes. Add thyme, bay leaf, salt, pepper, and stock. Bring to a low boil, then lower to a simmer and cover for 15 minutes, or until celery root is soft.

3. Add cubed fish. Cover and cook another 5 to 10 minutes, or until fish is opaque and flakes easily with a fork. Serve warm, garnished with parsley and reserved bacon.

Makes 4 to 6
servings

SCD
Paleo
GF
Nut-Free
DF option

Options:
* Substitute cooked diced turkey for the chicken.

Sweet potato is very high in nickel. Omit if you have a nickel allergy.

CHICKEN SOUP

This is a classic. My Italian grandmother Nani, always added sweet potato to deepen the flavors, add color, and thicken the soup.

1 Tbs olive oil or fat
1 large onion chopped
2 stalks of celery chopped
3 carrots chopped
2 garlic cloves sliced
Salt and Pepper to taste
3/4 cups cooked chicken*

1 large sweet potato diced
1 small bunch of Swiss chard
2 sprigs of fresh thyme
1 bay leaf
5 cups chicken broth
1/2 cup dried pea or lentil pasta
1/2 cup frozen peas

1. Heat oil in soup pot. Add onions and saute until transparent. Add garlic, celery and carrots. Saute until lightly browned.

2. Add sweet potato, Swiss chard, and herbs. Stir together, then add stock. Bring to a rolling boil, then lower heat to medium, cover, and cook 10 minutes.

3. Bring back to a simmer and add pea pasta, peas, and diced chicken. Simmer for 8 minutes, or until pasta and peas are soft. Serve with herbed biscuits if you like (*see p. 119*).

Tarragon Chicken Salad

I've always loved the flavor of tarragon. It pairs well with fruit.

Options:
This is also delicious with red grapes.

SCD option:
Omit sunflower seeds, and use cider vinegar in the dressing instead of balsamic vinegar.

2 boneless chicken breasts
1 Tbs butter or substitute
1/3 cup white wine or broth
1 Tbs fresh tarragon snipped
3 cups salad greens
1/4 cup balsamic vinaigrette *(p. 145)*

1 small red onion minced
1/4 cup mayonnaise *(p. 136)*
1 apple cored and chopped
1 avocado diced
toasted sunflower seeds

1. Poach chicken: In deep skillet with lid, melt butter over medium high heat. Add chicken breasts, and season with salt and pepper. Brown on both sides for 5 minutes, then add wine or broth and cover. Reduce heat to low and simmer for 15 minutes. Allow to cool completely and chop fine.

2. Place chopped chicken, tarragon, onion, and mayonnaise in a large mixing bowl. Toss to combine. Keep cool until ready to serve.

3. Place 3/4 cup of greens in each salad bowl. Divide chicken salad, apple, and avocado between bowls. Garnish with toasted sunflower seeds and drizzle with balsamic vinaigrette.⁎

**SCD
Paleo option
GF
Nut-Free
DF
Vegetarian**

Options:
* You may substitute 1 cup of dried navy beans for the canned beans. See cooking directions on page 13. Rinse before using.

Paleo Option:
Tomatoes and peppers are nightshades and can cause inflammation. Replace with cucumber and/or shredded carrot if you're sensitive.

Notes:
Lentil pasta is very high in nickel. Eat it sparingly if you have a nickel allergy.

Pasta & Bean Salad

Cold, vegetarian, and colorful – this makes a perfect potluck dish.

1 - 8oz box lentil rotini
1 - 15 oz. can navy beans*
1 small red onion, sliced
1 large scallion, sliced
salt and pepper to taste

1/2 colored pepper, chopped
1 cup cherry tomatoes, halved
1 cup fresh green beans, chopped
1/4 cup parsley, chopped
1/2 cup balsamic vinaigrette *(p. 145)*

1. Place canned navy beans in a colander and rinse until no longer foaming. Set aside to drain.*

2. Cook fresh green beans in a small sauce pan with 1/4 cup water and 1/4 tsp salt, until just soft. Drain and put aside.

3. Fill large pot with water and bring to a boil. Add 1/2 tsp salt, and dry rotini. Reduce heat to medium and simmer 7 minutes, or until just tender. Drain and rinse.

4. Place cooked rotini in a large mixing bowl and drizzle with 1/4 cup of vinaigrette. Toss to coat, and allow to sit until cool.

5. Add red onion, scallion, pepper, cherry tomatoe, green beans, parsley, remaining 1/4 cup vinaigrette, and canned navy beans to pasta in mixing bowl and toss to coat. Season to taste and serve with nasturtiums if available. Refrigerate any leftovers.

Egg Salad Stuffed Tomato

Makes
4 servings

SCD
GF
Nut-Free
DF
Low Nickel
Vegetarian

Note:

To hard boil eggs:
1. Place 4 eggs and 1/4 tsp salt in a medium-sized sauce pan. Cover with enough water so the eggs are at least 1" below the surface.

2. Bring to a rolling boil. Turn off the heat, and leave on the burner for 10 to 12 minutes.

3. Remove eggs from pan with a slotted spoon and place in a heat-poof bowl. Run cold water over the eggs to stop them continuing to cook.

4. Allow the eggs to cool before peeling.

I enjoy hosting a light lunch outside with friends during the summer. The creamy yellow of the egg salad and deep red of a garden ripe tomato create a refreshing and elegant side dish for a vegetarian luncheon. You can make the egg salad ahead of time and fill the prepared tomatoes just before serving.

4 large ripe tomatoes
4 hard boiled eggs peeled
1 small red onion
1 stalk celery diced
2 Tbs red pepper diced

1/4 cup homemade mayonnaise *(p. 136)*
2 Tbs fresh parsley chopped
1/4 tsp herb sea salt or to taste
1/4 tsp pepper
snipped chives for garnish

1. Cut out the stem end of each tomato in a cone shape and remove. Using a spoon remove the seeds and some of the inner membrane leaving a bowl shape. Place cut side down on a clean towel to drain.

2. Dice hard boiled eggs into a medium sized bowl. Peel onion and slice into 4 thin rings. Put aside for garnish. Mince 1 Tbs from the remaining onion, and add to bowl along with celery, pepper, mayonnaise, and seasonings. Stir to combine. Keep refrigerated until ready to serve.

3. Arrange tomatoes cut side up on individual salad plates. Fill with egg salad and garnish with chives and reserved onion.

Mediterranean Tuna Salad

Makes
4 servings

Paleo option
GF
Nut-Free
DF

Options:
More garnishes:
Cucumbers
Capers
Avocado
Pickled peppers
Roasted peppers

Paleo option:
substitute cucumbers
and avocado for the
roasted tomatoes and
peppers.

Note:
If you have a nickel
allergy be sure to
use tuna sold in glass
jars.

Check the ingre-
dients in prepared
foods and avoid
sugars or starches if
following the SCD
diet.

This salad is a great lunch staple for the winter months. It's quick and easy to throw together from items you can keep stocked in the cupboard.

1 - 6 oz. jar of tuna in oil
8 roasted tomatoes in oil
1 small red onion sliced thin
1/2 cup Creamy Vinaigrette Dressing *(pg. 145)*

8 roasted artichoke hearts sliced
1/4 cup kalamata olives, pitted
4-6 cups mixed salad greens

1. Place mixed greens in a serving bowl or in individual salad bowls. Add tuna, and garnishes of your choice and drizzle with the dressing.

2. Serve immediately. Refrigerate any leftovers.

PEA GREEN SALAD

SCD
Paleo
GF
Nut-Free
DF
Vegetarian

Notes:
Pea greens are very high in nickel. Eat them sparingly if you have a nickel allergy.

What do you do with those sprightly pea greens? Let their flavor shine by adding a bit of red onion and a light drizzle of creamy vinaigrette.

4 cups of loosely packed fresh pea greens
4 rings of red onion, thinly sliced
1/4 cup creamy vinaigrette *(p. 145)*

1. Wash and spin pea greens. Place pea greens in individual salad bowls, or a serving bowl.

2. Break onion slices into rings and place on top of pea greens.

3. Drizzle salad with creamy vinaigrette and serve immediately.

SCD
Paleo
GF
Nut-Free
DF
Vegetarian

Options:
You may substitute: Green cabbage for the red cabbage, and fruit juice sweetened dried cranberries for the raisins.

Confetti Salad

Colorful, and easy to prepare ahead of time, this salad makes a great vegetarian side dish for a potluck or luncheon with friends.

Salad:

1/4 red cabbage sliced thin
1 apple shredded
2 stalks celery sliced
1 cup raisins
2 large carrots shredded
1 small red onion minced
1/4 tsp salt & pepper

Dressing:

1 1/2 Tbs balsamic vinegar
1 1/2 Tbs honey
1/8 tsp salt & pepper
1 Tbs homemade mayonnaise *(p. 136)*
1/4 cup sunflower oil

1. Mix together salad ingredients in a large serving bowl.

2. In a small bowl mix together the vinegar, mayonnaise, honey, salt, and pepper. Whisk in the sunflower oil in a thin stream. Pour dressing over the salad and toss before serving. Refrigerate any leftovers.

FORAGING Adventures

When I was a toddler, my parents built a house on a 100 acre chunk of paradise in CT. My brother and I grew up roaming through the oak and pine forests, building stick bridges over the streams, and foraging.

My grandmother adored the wild blueberries that clung thickly to the granite outcropping we called Snake Face Rock. She endured hours in the heat filling dixie cups with the tiny berries. I loved the challenge of finding the biggest, sweetest berries, but most ended up in my mouth rather than my dixie cup.

I remember when my father pointed out the wild strawberries in the grass along the path to our pond. I quickly learned to identify the strawberry leaves, and with my close proximity to the ground, had great success plucking these bumpy red treats. Looking back now, I was so fortunate to be introduced to foraging at such a young age. It has taught me the knack of identifying plants by leaf, habitat, scent, and growth habit. Over the years, I've nurtured these skills through books, walks with foraging friends, and experience. It's very important to get confirmation from an experienced forager, and check to be sure the area hasn't been sprayed with herbicides or pesticides before eating anything from the wild. But the joys of finding food growing in a natural environment is a wonderful experience for a young person.

In late summer of 2019 a group of enthusiastic homeschooled teens joined me for a Farm, Forage, Fire class. We spent weeks visiting our local woods, fields, coastline and farms. We gathered fox grapes, jewel weed pods, hickory nuts, black walnuts, autumn olive berries, wintergreen, beach plums, wild cranberries, locally grown apples, lima beans, greens, chocolate mint, edible flowers, chicken, and cream. We learned about sustainable agriculture practices at our local farms. Our feast on the last day of class was cooked over a fire. Our goal was to produce a menu without any foods from a grocery store. Each student used what we had gathered to create a dish. The meal was abundant, meaningful and delicious.

One cold Spring morning, Frederick and I discovered maple icicles. The sparkle of the droplets of sap caught our eye as we finished our farm chores. Russ Oliviera, the farm manager, had recently cut some red maple branches overhanging the dirt drive. As the spring sun warmed the tree trunk the previous day, the sap began to run from the roots up into the branch tips. The cool night had frozen the sap, and created cascades of maple icicles. We climbed up on the truck bed, snapped the icicles off and crunched on the sweet treats. This began an annual ritual of tapping red maple trees. In the absence of sugar maples, red maples makes a delightful root beer flavored syrup. The year we discovered the icicles, a drought the previous summer had concentrated the tree sap. Some years, the sap is more diluted, and needs to be boiled down longer. After several days simmering on the wood stove, the sap is moved to the stove top for finishing. We carefully ration out the pint or so of syrup we make each year, occasionally forcing a spoonful onto unsuspecting visitors, who exclaim at the intense flavor.

The day I met Eva Sommeripa, she put a giant yogurt container on a string around my neck and inducted me into her foraging family. She came to our farm to forage for berries, and we hit the jackpot! The blackberry bushes had taken over the edges of an old farm lane, and we spent many happy hours filling our baskets. Over the years Eva has taught me the joys of autumn olive, glasswort, beach rose hips and American redbud blossoms. She's created an entire business around edible weeds, flowers, greens, and foraged plants. Eva's Garden is legendary among chefs and restaurant owners across New England. She has introduced many to the joys of wild edibles and unusual flavor experiences.

My friend, Bette Low is another fellow forager. We schedule our foraging walks to destinations with wild cranberries, fox grapes, morels, and beech nuts. I remember tramping through a dense pitch pine forest and discovering an old cranberry bog crusted over with ice. We collected a good haul before our fingers and booted feet became numb with cold. I remember the delicious cranberry bread I made from those chilly berries.

One year, Bette hosted a Boston Mycological Society meeting. These mushroom hunters were serious about their foraging. After a brief introduction, we all melted into the woods, carrying baskets. We collected a small sample of anything we discovered, no matter if it was poisonous or edible. Upon our return, the members got to work, sorting and arranging the group's collection. They spread the mushrooms out on old planks according to their taxonomy. The gorgeous array of fungi with their subtle and intense colors, waxy and shingled textures, and various sizes were spectacular to behold.

Frederick's favorite wild food is the beach plum. These plump purple berries are a bit too tart to eat straight, but simmer them down and mix them with honey, and they create a uniquely flavored syrup. The trick to beach plum hunting is to look for the flowering bushes in spring. When you return in the late summer, prepare to battle paper wasp nests, mosquitoes and poison ivy. Frederick is very secretive about his foraging spots, and he guards their locations ferociously.

VEGETABLES

RED CABBAGE WITH APPLES

This side dish goes well with pork and wild game.

SCD option
Paleo option
GF
Nut-Free
Low Nickel
DF option

Options:
SCD & Paleo:
Use dairy-free butter.

My mother adds a cheese cloth bag with 1 Tbs of pickling spices to this recipe while it simmers. Remove the bag before serving.

1 medium sized red cabbage, sliced thin
1 Tbs butter or substitute
1 cooking apple peeled and diced
1 small onion or shallot chopped
1 Tbs sherry vinegar
1 Tbs honey
2 Tbs of water, more as needed
1 bay leaf
salt and pepper to taste

1. Melt butter in a large covered saucepan on medium high heat. Add onions saute until transparent. Add apples and cabbage and stir to combine. Saute for 5 minutes.

2. Add vinegar, water, bay leaf, salt and pepper. Cook with the cover on for 15 to 20 minutes, stirring every 5 minutes. Add more water if needed.

3. When cabbage is wilted and dark purple, remove cover and continue cooking until the remaining liquid evaporates. Remove bay leaf. Serve warm. Refrigerate any leftovers.

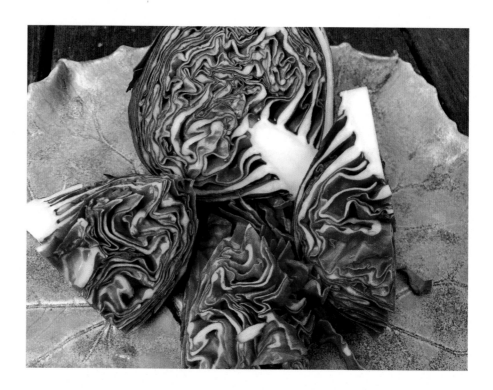

SCD option
Paleo option
GF
Nut-Free
DF option

Options:
SCD & Paleo:
Use dairy-free butter.

* You can also substitute garlic for the onion but omit the nutmeg, and replace with 1/4 tsp. of cayanne pepper, or to taste.

Notes:
Kale, collards, beet greens and Swiss chard are moderately high in nickel. Eat them sparingly if you have a nickel allergy.

BRAISED GREENS

I never understood how good cooked greens could be until I learned this cooking method.

1 large bunch of kale, collards, beet greens, or Swiss chard
1 small onion or shallot*   1/2 tsp nutmeg
2 Tbs butter or substitute   salt and pepper to taste
2 Tbs white wine, chicken broth, or water
Toasted sunflower seeds for garnish *(p. 149) optional*

1. Rinse greens well and chop into bite-sized pieces.

2. Heat 12" covered skillet on medium-high heat. Add butter and onions and saute until transparent. Add greens and white wine and cover. Braise for 10 to 15 minutes, until greens are soft. Remove cover and let the remaining liquid evaporate. Add seasonings. Serve topped with toasted sunflower seeds.

ROASTED CARROTS & BEETS

Roasting makes beets sweet and tender.

SCD
Paleo
GF
Nut-Free
DF option

Options:
You can roast a variety of root vegetables this way. Try adding parsnips, turnips, leeks or radishes.

3 medium beets scrubbed
4-5 thick carrots
5 shallots peeled and cut in half
1 Tbs fresh rosemary leaves
1 Tbs olive oil
salt and pepper to taste

1. Preheat oven to 400° F.

2. Cut ends off beets and carrots, and cut in even bite-sized pieces. Add shallots and rosemary and place in a pile in the center of a large rimmed baking pan. Drizzle with olive oil, and sprinkle with salt and pepper. Toss well to coat. Spread out evenly in pan.

3. Place baking pan in preheated oven and roast 30 to 45 minutes or until vegetables are soft and lightly browned.

4. Serve warm or at room temperature.

Makes 4 to 6
servings

SCD
GF
Nut-Free
DF option

Options:
* If you can't find
shallots, you may
substitute 1 red onion.

Note:
** To reduce in-
flammation, remove
tomato seeds before
cooking, then remove
skins before serving.

Green beans are
moderately high in
nickel. Eat them
sparingly if you have
a nickel allergy.

GREEN BEANS WITH CUMIN

Thanks go to my brother Paul for this delicious rendition of green beans.

2 cups green beans washed and cut into bite-sized pieces
3 shallots peeled and sliced*
2 tsp ground cumin
2 Tbs olive oil divided
salt and pepper to taste
2 Tbs chicken broth, or water
10 cherry tomatoes halved**

1. Heat 12" covered skillet on medium-high heat. Add 1 Tbs olive oil and shallots. Saute until caramelized and crispy. Remove from pan and spread out on paper towel to keep crisp.

2. Add cumin and the remaining 1 Tbs olive oil to the pan and stir to incorporate. Add green beans, tomatoes, salt, pepper, and chicken broth or water. Cover and steam for 10 minutes, or until green beans are just tender. Remove cover and let most of the remaining liquid evaporate.

3. Adjust seasonings. Serve topped with crispy shallots.

ROASTED TOMATOES

This is a wonderful way to process vast quantities of garden tomatoes.

**SCD
GF
Nut-Free
DF option**

ROASTED TOMATO SAUCE

Using food processor, puree cooled roasted tomatoes, with any accumulated juices, until smooth. Refrigerate in glass container for up to 1 week, or freeze for up to 6 months.

Note:
*To reduce inflammation, remove seeds from halved tomatoes before cooking, then remove skins before using.

5 lbs. fresh tomatoes (a variety of paste and heirloom)*
1 Tbs olive oil   3 cloves garlic sliced
1 Tbs balsamic vinegar   1 small onion minced
1 1/2 tsp sea salt   1/2 tsp pepper
2 tsp each of dried oregano, basil and thyme

1. Preheat oven to 400° F.

2. Using 1 or 2 large-rimmed glass baking (lasagna) pans, or other non-reactive pan, spread olive oil, balsamic vinegar, onion, garlic and seasonings evenly on the bottom.

3. Wash tomatoes, cut in half lengthwise, and remove stem ends. Place tomatoes cut side down and space evenly in pan(s).

3. Place baking pans in preheated oven and roast 40 minutes. Remove pan(s) from oven and using wooden (or non-reactive) tongs flip tomatoes so they are cut side up. Continue roasting for another 30 to 35 minutes more, or until tomatoes are soft and juices in the bottom of the pans are thickened.

4. Serve warm or at room temperature in salads, or make into tomato sauce (see side bar). Store any remaining tomatoes in a glass or non-reactive container in the refrigerator for up to 1 week. Can also be frozen for up to 6 months.

SCD
Paleo
GF
Nut-Free
DF option

Options:
* You can replace the
shallots with 1 small
red onion.

Note: If you
can tolerate dairy,
sprinkle 1/2 cup of
crumbled goat cheese
or chevre before
serving. It is a deli-
cious addition.

Winter squash is
moderately high in
nickel. Eat it spar-
ingly if you have a
nickel allergy.

ROASTED BUTTERNUT SQUASH

I love the peeled and cubed local butternut squash available in our market.
If you don't have access to this convenience, use caution peeling, cutting,
and removing seeds.

1 — 18 oz. package of cubed butternut squash
2 shallots sliced*   1 Tbs olive oil
salt and pepper to taste   1 Tbs fresh parsley chopped
1/4 cup fruit juice sweetened dried cranberries
toasted sunflower seeds for garnish *(p. 149)*

1. Preheat oven to 400° F.

2. Line a baking sheet with parchment paper and place squash, shallots,
salt, and pepper in the center. Drizzle with olive oil, and toss to coat. Spread
out ingredients evenly, and roast for 30 to 40 minutes, or until edges are
lightly browned, and the squash is soft.

3. Remove from oven and place in a serving bowl with dried cranberries,
and parsley and toss together. Adjust seasonings. Serve topped with toasted
sunflower seeds.

ZUCCHINI FRITTERS

The crispy edges and savory flavors of these fritters make them a great side dish for hearty meats or fish.

SCD option
Paleo
GF
Nut-Free
DF

Options:
You can also add 1/4 cup grated Parmesan cheese to the batter if you can tolerate dairy.

SCD option:
Substitute almond flour for flax meal.

For Breakfast:
Reheat any leftover fritters at 400° F for 8 minutes and serve topped with poached or fried eggs.

Note:
This is a good way to use up overgrown zucchini.

1 large zucchini (2 cups shredded)
1 large onion
1 clove garlic minced
1/4 cup flax meal
1/4 cup coconut flour
1/2 Tbs each fresh oregano and parsley, chopped or 1 tsp dried

4 large eggs
1 tsp herbed salt
1/4 tsp freshly ground pepper
2 Tbs olive oil
1 tsp salt

1. Shred zucchini and onion in a food processor. Place them in a colander, toss with 1 tsp salt and drain for 15 minutes. Squeeze out any liquid.

2. To make the batter, combine eggs with herbs, garlic, salt and pepper in a large bowl. Whisk well to combine. Add flax meal, coconut flour, grated zucchini and onion. Mix well using a spoon or your hands.

3. Heat olive oil in a 12" skillet over medium-high heat. Scoop up a 1/4 cup of batter and drain out any moisture. Carefully drop batter into oil, and flatten to 1/4" with a spatula. Brown on both sides. This should take approximately 3 to 5 minutes on each side.

4. Serve warm topped with tomato, shredded basil, and pesto mayonnaise *(p. 124)* or warm tomato sauce.

Sweet Potato Puree

Makes 3 to 4 servings

**Paleo option
GF
Nut-Free
DF option**

Options:
Paleo option:
Use dairy-free butter.

❋ You can substitute pumpkin or winter squash for the sweet potato.

Notes:
Sweet potato is very high in nickel. Eat it sparingly if you have a nickel allergy.

I like to bake a few extra sweet potatoes so I can make this with the leftovers.

2 large sweet potatoes   salt and pepper to taste
2 Tbs butter or substitute

1. Preheat oven to 400° F. Rinse sweet potatoes and poke top with a knife. Space evenly on glass or ceramic baking dish and roast for 30 to 45 minutes until very soft.

2. Allow to cool briefly. Remove and discard the skins and dice the sweet potato into the bowl of a food processor. Add butter and salt and pepper to taste and process until smooth. If too dry add a bit of water and continue blending. *If you don't have a food processor you can mix in a bowl with a fork, pastry blender, or whisk.*

3. Place in small baking dish and bake at 350° F for approximately 10 minutes or until warmed through.

BACON -STUFFED MUSHROOMS

1 small red onion chopped
1/2 apple peeled and diced
2 slices of uncooked bacon chopped*
1 stalk celery chopped
1/2 Tbs each of fresh thyme, rosemary, sage and parsley leaves

2 Tbs flax meal
1/2 tsp herbed salt
1/4 tsp freshly ground pepper
16 oz. white mushrooms**

SCD option
Paleo
GF
Nut-Free
DF

Options:

This stuffing can also be used to stuff chicken breasts, turkey tenderloins, or fish fillets.

Note:

*Sugar-free bacon.

**Use only very fresh mushrooms, and do not wash them. Any water will be absorbed, and make the stuffing soggy. Instead, remove any soil with your fingers or a soft brush.

SCD option: substitute 2 Tbls each almond flour and coconut flour for the flax meal.

1. Brush any soil off the mushrooms, and trim off stem ends. Remove stems from caps and put aside mushroom caps for later.

To Make Stuffing:
1. Chop the mushroom stems, along with 1 or 2 mushroom caps. Place chopped mushroom stems and remaining ingredients in a food processor. Pulse until small chunks remain.

To Stuff Mushrooms:
1. Preheat oven to 400° F.

2. Place enough stuffing to fill each mushroom cap. Place stuffed side up on rimmed sheet pan lined with parchment, or greased glass baking dish. Don't over crowd the 'shrooms.

3. Bake for 20 to 30 minutes, or until mushrooms are well cooked and tops are lightly browned. Cool slightly before serving.

Notes:
* dried Italian herbs
are a mixture of dried
parsley, oregano,
basil, and thyme.

Avocado is very high
in nickel. Eat it spar-
ingly if you have a
nickel allergy.

PORTOBELLO MUSHROOMS

These make a wonderful vegetarian meal.

Marinade:
1 Tbs balsamic vinegar
2 Tbs olive oil
2 large portobello mushrooms

1/2 tsp dried Italian herbs*
1 clove garlic minced
salt and pepper to taste

Toppings:
1 red onion sliced
1/2 red pepper sliced
3 Tbs garlic mayonnaise *(pg. 136)*

1 Tbs olive oil
1/2 avocado sliced

1. To make marinade mix together balsamic vinegar, olive oil, herbs, garlic, salt and pepper. Place mushrooms gill sides up on a plate and spoon marinade evenly over the top. Let mushrooms sit, gill sides up, for 30 minutes at room temperature.

2. Meanwhile, heat a skillet over medium high heat. Add olive oil, red onion and red pepper. Saute for 8 minutes, or until onions are browned and red pepper is soft. Remove and keep warm.

3. In the same skillet place mushrooms gill side up. Saute on both sides for 5 to 7 minutes, or until browned and mushrooms are soft. Place on serving dish. Top with sauted onions and peppers. Just before serving, add avocado and 11/2 Tbs of garlic mayonnaise on top of each. Garnish with parsley.

CRUNCHY SNAP PEAS

Options:
SCD & Paleo:
Use dairy-free butter.

Notes:
The key to crunchy snap peas is the timing. Be sure to cook them just before serving, and when in doubt under cook them.

Peas are very high in nickel. Eat them sparingly if you have a nickel allergy.

If you have a garden and grow peas, consider including sugar snap peas. They are easy, prolific, and delicious, fresh or lightly sauted. They are also readily available at farmers markets in Spring and Autumn.

2 cups fresh snap peas, washed
1 Tbs herb butter *(pg. 138)*
1/2 tsp salt
1 Tbs water
1 fresh scallion, white parts sliced thin

1. Cut through the stem end of snap peas, and peel off and discard any strings.

2. Preheat lidded saute pan on medium-high heat. Melt herb butter and add snap peas, scallion, salt and 1 Tbs water and cover with lid immediately.

3. Turn heat down to medium and let simmer for 1 to 2 minutes, or until peas turn bright green, but are still very firm.

4. Remove cover. Saute 1 minute more or until most of the liquid has evaporated. Serve immediately, as the snap peas will continue to cook as they sit.

Roasted Acorn Squash

These make a nice side dish to pork and turkey dishes.

1 large acorn squash*
2 Tbs butter or substitute softened
2 Tbs honey
1/2 tsp. nutmeg
salt and pepper to taste

1. Preheat oven to 400° F. Rinse acorn squash and poke top with a knife. Place in heat-proof glass or ceramic baking dish and roast for 30 to 45 minutes until very soft.

2. While acorn squash is roasting, mix together remaining ingredients in a small bowl. Put aside.

3. Remove squash from oven. Allow to cool briefly and cut in half. Remove the seeds and place cut side up in a baking dish. Spread the top cut surface all over with honey and butter mixture.

4. Return baking dish to the oven and continue roasting for 10 to 15 minutes, or until nicely browned. Once cooled slightly, they may be cut in half to serve 4, or served whole to serve 2.

SCD option
Paleo option
GF
Nut-Free
DF option

Options:
SCD & Paleo:
Use dairy-free butter.

* You can also substitute sweet momma squash, pumpkin, or any other small winter squash for the acorn squash. Adjust cooking time and ingredients accordingly.

Notes:
Winter squash is moderately high in nickel. Eat it sparingly if you have a nickel allergy.

74

RUSTIC *Meats*

During a Trompe l'oiel painting class at Rhode Island School of Design's headquarters in Italy, I learned how to really cook a chicken. I have pet chickens, and while I tend to avoid eating chicken because I consider them family now, back then, I had no reservations. My professor Jean Blackburn had taught me about the wonders of whole fresh chicken from the Italian markets on Federal Hill in Providence, RI. In her scientific illustration class she had us cook a whole chicken (head, neck, feet and all). We proceeded to remove all the bones, and reconstruct the skeleton using hot glue then drew it to scale. This was very educational, but no easy task. So when some friends had the idea of buying a chicken and roasting it in the kitchen at our Pensione, they turned to me as the expert. We had been subsisting on a student's diet, which in Italy consisted of a lot of very delicious pasta and pizza. However a simple home roasted chicken sounded very tempting.

Early the next morning, my roommate Sprout and I were dispatched to the morning market for carrots, onions and celery. Our friends had the difficult task of visiting the butcher to bring home the chicken. The kitchen was a delightful nook full of shelves, old wooden tables and stone walls with a few clouded windows that let in a bit of light. I unwrapped the paper from our bird and surveyed my task. Luckily, this time there was no head for me to contend with, but I still needed to find a sharp knife to prepare the bird. After careful cleaning and rinsing, I seasoned it with dried sage, salt, and pepper. We tucked it into a pan (breast side down) atop the carrots, onions, and celery, drizzled it with olive oil and popped it in a slow oven. The smell coming from the kitchen that afternoon was like ambrosia.

On the same trip we visited a restaurant decked out in red and white checked tablecloths with candles stuffed into rafia wrapped wine bottles. The decor was rather cliché, but the food was very good. I ordered pigeon, in an effort to be adventurous. I must say it was really delicious. However once we picked up our full bellies and walked out onto the sidewalk, I had the strangest feeling while walking among the pigeons. They seemed to be eyeing me with a rather knowing look, and my feelings of guilt prevented me from eating pigeon again.

While staying on Pasque Island with some friends, we took turns preparing meals. We brought all of our food with us to this remote spot, and found the gas powered refrigerator was not only rather small, but didn't seem to keep things very cool. There was a rush to eat the wilting kale, and limp green beans. But the fishing was extraordinary, which ironically produced the best venison I've ever eaten. Our friend Dale brought some venison steaks and a small

wood fired camp stove. He marinated the venison in mustard, honey, soy, ginger, and red wine. We dutifully let it sit over night. However over the next three days the fishing was so good, the venison continued to sit in it's bath in the cold-est part of the fridge we could find. Day 4 came to a close and I suggested we cook the venison, despite the striped bass sitting on the counter. Dale started up the wood fired grill, and sat in the murky dusk flipping it over and over. After letting it cool for a few minutes he sliced it thinly and arranged it on one of the oval ironware plates. We passed it around, and marveled at it's buttery tenderness and rich flavors.

For many years we migrated with the birds to Monhegan Island in Maine. The warblers would arrive on west winds, and flop at our feet; they were so exhausted from their trav-els. Bird watching was just too easy. No, we never ate the warblers, but the lobster was a different story. Fred went down to the docks when my family came for a visit. He and my father bought more than half a dozen lobsters from a neighbor's boat. The Pratt cottage where we were staying, did not have electricity, nor did it have heat. The warmest place tended to be next to or above the gas powered refrigerator. Unfortunately the kitchen table (next to said fridge) was too small for the 6 of us. Once our lobsters were boiled, and my father had split them, we brought them and the melted butter out onto the deck to watch the sun set. The first few mouthfuls were succulent, however the chilly air soon congealed the butter so that we were scooping butter up with the chunks of lobster. I have to say the additional amounts of butter consumed this way did not detract from the lobster at all. Once we were satiated, and the sun crawled below the waves, we retired to the liv-ing room fire, to warm up and play a game of cards.

On his way home from work one spring evening, Frederick saw a wild turkey get hit by a car in front of him. The turkey died a quick death, and Frederick decided to bring it home. I refused to clean it, having by that time developed an affection for these birds who wandered through our yard. We called Bette, and she picked it up the next day. She made quick work of the plucking and preparing and had it roasting in the oven by the time her husband Ed got home. There is a reason spring turkeys aren't popular. They've made it through the winter subsisting on beech nuts, and acorns and are generally thin and tough by the time the weather warms. Ed claims they could barely cut the meat, and chewing was impossible. The cooked turkey meat was offered the next day to Blue, their dog. After some valiant attempts, even Blue gave up. Some things just aren't meant to be eaten.

PROTEINS

BRAISED BEEF SHORT RIBS

SCD
Paleo
GF
Nut-Free
DF

Options:

*You may use 3 lbs of bone-in beef short ribs.

Note:

I put the herb sprigs in whole, and let the cooking process separate the leaves from the stems. Remove any stems, along with fat and bones, before serving.

Short ribs are comfort food. The long cooking time makes them succulent.

2 lbs boneless beef short ribs*
3 Tbs olive oil
1 onion chopped
3 cloves of garlic sliced
2 carrots cut in chunks
1 bay leaf

1 sprig of winter savory
1 sprig of rosemary
2 sprigs of thyme
1 tsp each sea salt & pepper
1 1/2 cups beef broth or water
1/4 cup red wine or water

1. Preheat oven to 350° F.

2. Season all sides of ribs with salt and pepper.

3. On stove top heat oven-proof Dutch oven over medium-high heat. Add olive oil and sear ribs for 1 minute on all sides. Remove and keep warm on a plate.

4. Lower heat to medium and add onions and garlic. Saute for 5 minutes, then add carrots, herbs, salt and pepper. Return ribs and any accumulated juices to pot, along with broth and red wine. Cover and place in oven for 2 1/2 to 3 hours.

5. Remove any fat and bones, and shred the meat. Serve with the onions, garlic, carrots, and some of the broth over white bean rosemary mash, or steamed cauliflower.

SCD
Paleo
GF
Nut-Free
DF

Options:
You may substitute other herbs for the thyme & rosemary, depending on the seasonings in the accompanying foods.

Notes:
Short on time? You can substitute two 15 oz cans of rinsed navy beans for the dried beans and proceed with the recipe from step 2.

Beans are very high in nickel. Eat them sparingly if you have a nickel allergy.

WHITE BEAN ROSEMARY MASH

This is a delicious substitute for mashed potatoes, and good as a base for meat dishes with sauces.

1 1/2 cups dried navy beans
2 Tbs olive oil
2 cloves of garlic minced
1 cup broth or water, plus more water for soaking

1 large sprig of rosemary
2 sprigs of thyme
1 tsp sea salt or to taste

1. The night before, place the navy beans in a deep soup pot. Cover with 4 cups of water. Bring to a boil. Turn off heat, and leave to soak over night.

2. 1 hour before serving, pour beans in a colander and rinse well. Set aside to drain.

3. Heat a 12" skillet over medium heat. Saute garlic for a minute or two, then add herbs and rinsed beans. Add 1 cup of broth or water and salt. Cover and simmer for 1/2 hour or more, adding water if it gets dry.

3. As the beans get soft, mash gently with the back of a spoon or spatula. Serve warm.

FRIED FISH

Options:
*Substitute fluke, haddock, cod, sea bass, or other white fish for the halibut.

**No lemon balm? Substitute 1/2 tsp mixed Italian herbs.

SCD Option:
Use 2 Tbs coconut flour, and omit the flax meal.

The key to crispy fried fish is high heat and beaten egg whites. This dish works with many kinds of thick white fish fillets.

2 medium halibut fillets*
2 egg whites
1 Tbs coconut flour
1 Tbs golden flax meal

4 lemon balm leaves chopped**
1 - 2 Tbs water
2 - 3 Tbs sunflower oil
1/4 tsp each sea salt and pepper

1. If fish is thicker than 1", cut fillets into 1" strips across the grain. Use thinner fillets whole.

2. Beat egg whites to soft peaks and stir in coconut flour, sea salt, pepper and lemon balm. Let sit for 5 minutes. Batter should be just loose enough to coat the fillets. If too stiff, add enough water to make a batter.

3. Preheat deep 12" skillet on medium high heat. Add olive oil. Coat fish fillets with batter one at a time. Fry until nicely browned on both sides, and fish flakes easily with a fork. Serve immediately with herb mayonnaise *(p. 124)* or homemade ketchup *(p. 125)*.

**SCD option
Paleo
GF
Nut-Free
DF**

Options:
*Types of Fish:
blue fish, tautog, cod,
swordfish, halibut,
black sea bass, or
other white fish.

SCD option:
Substitute almond
flour for flax meal.

Note:
A squeeze of lemon
juice after baking is
nice if you can have
it.

Baked Fish

This is a good way to bake any thick white fish.

3 fish fillets*
3 Tbs golden flax meal
1 1/2 Tbs coconut flour
1/2 tsp mixed dried herbs
1/4 tsp sea salt
Freshly ground pepper
1/4 cup homemade garlic mayonnaise *(p. 136)*

1. Preheat oven to 350° F. In a small bowl mix together dry ingredients and put aside.

2. Place filets (skin side down if they have skin) evenly spaced in a low, heat-proof glass baking dish. Coat the tops with mayonnaise, and sprinkle with flax mixture.

3. Bake at 350° F for 10 to 15 minutes or until fish flakes easily with a fork.

CHICKEN CURRY WITH FRUIT

Serves 4

Paleo option
GF
Nut-Free
DF

Options:
Paleo option:
Use dairy-free butter.

*If you don't have fresh cilantro, you can use parsley or 2 tsp dried, but the flavor won't be the same.

**or apricots.

An Elegant Luncheon:
Use this as a filling in crepes. Place 1/3 cup in the center and fold crepe like an envelope. Then place fold side down in buttered baking dish, and brush the tops with melted butter. Bake at 350° F, until crepes are lightly browned and filling is bubbling, 15 to 20 minutes.
See crepe recipe on p. 139.

83

2 boneless chicken breasts*
1/4 cup white wine
1/4 tsp sea salt
5 slices dried mango**
2 Tbs herb butter, divided
3 shallots, peeled and diced
2 Tbs curry powder
1 tsp chives   (fresh or dried)
2 Tbs fresh cilantro, divided*
1/3 cup chicken broth
1 Tbs herb butter
freshly ground pepper
1/2 cup boiling water
1 apple peeled and diced
2 ripe bananas peeled and diced
1/4 tsp herbed sea salt
1/4 cup coconut milk
1/4 cup toasted unswtd. coconut

1. Place dried mango in a heat-proof bowl, and pour boiling water over to cover. Let sit 1/2 hour. When softened, dice mango and put aside with soaking liquid.

2. Melt 1 Tbs herb butter in 12" covered skillet over medium-high heat. Add chicken breasts, season with salt and pepper, and brown lightly for about 5 minutes on both sides. Lower heat to medium low, and add broth and white wine. Cover and simmer for 15 minutes. Remove chicken breasts to a plate and liquid from pan to a heat-proof bowl, and reserve. When slightly cooled, dice chicken.

3. Melt remaining 1 Tbs herb butter in skillet over medium heat, and saute shallots for 5 minutes. Add curry powder, apple, banana, mango (without juice), herbed salt, chives, and 1 Tbs cilantro and saute until fruit breaks down. Add juice from mango and cooking liquid from chicken, and simmer until reduced, and sauce is thickened. Stir in diced chicken and coconut milk and heat through. Serve garnished with toasted coconut and additional 1 Tbs cilantro.

BEEF BROCCOLI CURRY

Options:
Paleo:
Omit tomato.

Note:
*Coconut aminos may contain coconut sugar. If you are having issues with inflammation, you may want to avoid this.

**When using fresh plum tomatoes, peel and seed to reduce inflammation

This is a quick and easy stir-fried curry dish.

1 1/2 lbs. flank steak or stew beef cut in very thin strips.
1 Tbs toasted sesame seed oil
1 Tbs coconut aminos*

2 Tbs sunflower oil or duck fat, divided
2 Tbs curry powder
1 large onion sliced
1 large tomato diced**
1/4 tsp sea salt
1/4 cup white wine or water

1/2 green pepper seeded and diced
1 head broccoli cut in bite-sized pieces
1 Tbs honey
1 Tbs black sesame seeds

1. Mix together sesame oil and coconut aminos and marinate beef strips for 15 minutes.

2. Heat 1 Tbs oil over high heat in a 12" skillet, add curry powder and beef. Stir fry for 5 minutes, or until no longer pink. Remove to a bowl.

3. Add remaining 1 Tbs oil to skillet, and stir fry onion, broccoli, and green pepper for 5 minutes. Add tomato, honey, salt, and white wine. Reduce heat to medium high and simmer until liquid is reduced to a thick sauce.

4. Lower heat and add beef and up to 1 Tbs of reserved juices, and heat through. Serve garnished with sesame seeds.

WHITE BEAN CHILI

SCD
GF
Nut-Free
DF option

Options:
Diced zucchini is a nice addition.

Other Garnishes:
Plain coconut yogurt
Sliced green olives
Sliced scallions

Notes:
If you'd rather avoid the canned foods, you can substitute: 2 lbs. fresh plum tomatoes, diced, and 1 1/2 cups dried navy beans soaked over night in 6 cups water. Increase cooking time as needed to thicken before returning the beef or turkey to the pot.

Beans are very high in nickel. Eat them sparingly if you have a nickel allergy.

2 Tbs olive oil, divided
1 lb. ground beef or turkey
1 1/2 Tbs chili powder
1 Tbs cumin ground
1 large onion chopped
2 cloves garlic minced
2 stalks celery chopped
2 large carrots chopped

28 oz can fire-roasted tomatoes
2-15 oz cans navy beans, rinsed
1/2 cup red wine
1 cup tomato puree
1 Tbs Dijon mustard
1 tsp each dried basil and thyme
1/2 tsp dried oregano
1 1/2 tsp herbed sea salt

1 green bell pepper chopped freshly ground pepper to taste
1 bunch of fresh cilantro chopped for garnish

1. In a deep soup pot, heat 1 Tbs oil over medium-high heat. Add chili powder and ground cumin. Swirl to mix. Add crumbled ground beef or turkey. Stir, breaking up any chunks and cook until lightly browned. Remove to a bowl.

2. In the same pot, add remaining 1 Tbs oil, and saute onion and garlic for 5 minutes. Add celery, carrots, and peppers, and saute for 10 minutes or until softened. Add tomatoes, beans, red wine, tomato puree, mustard, herbs, salt, and pepper.

3. Stir well and simmer for 30 minutes to 1 hour to mix flavors.

4. Approximately 15 minutes before serving, add ground beef or turkey and heat through. Serve garnished with fresh cilantro.

Note:

Suggested sauces:
- Tartar Sauce
- Dill Sauce
- Pesto Mayonnaise
- Tomato Sauce
- Ketchup
- Mango chutney
- Cranberry Sauce

See Basics & Extras section for recipes.

*dried mixed herbs: I use equal parts dried parsley, thyme, basil, and oregano.

CHICKEN FINGERS

These are popular with kids of all ages.

2 chicken breasts
3 Tbs golden flax meal
1 tsp dried mixed herbs*
freshly ground pepper

1/2 cup garlic mayonnaise *(p. 136)*
3 Tbs coconut flour
1/4 tsp herbed sea salt

1. Preheat oven to 375° F. Line a sheet pan with parchment paper, and put aside.

2. In a shallow bowl mix together flax meal, coconut flour, herbs, salt and pepper. Put aside.

3. Cut chicken breasts across the grain in to 1 1/4" strips. Place the mayonnaise on the center of a plate. Using a rubber spatula, spread each chicken piece with mayonnaise, then coat with topping. Place on prepared sheet pan. When all pieces are coated, sprinkle any bare spots with remaining coating.

4. Bake chicken fingers for 10 minutes, turn over, and bake for an additional 5 to 10 minutes, or until cooked through, and nicely browned on both sides.

5. Serve with your choice of sauces. See sidebar.

86

Turkey Stuffed with Sage

SCD
Paleo
GF
Nut-Free
DF
Low Nickel

Options:
*You may also use chicken breasts for this recipe.

This is particularly nice in autumn served with roasted acorn squash and braised greens. Homemade cranberry sauce is a nice addition *(pg. 143)*.

2 medium turkey tenderloins*
1 Tbs duck fat
1/3 cup white wine, or broth
1/4 tsp each salt, pepper, and ground dried sage

2 slices of sugar free bacon
4 fresh sage leaves

1. Place turkey tenderloins on cutting board. With a sharp knife carefully remove white tendon from the center of the tenderloin. Continue cut leaving 1" attached so that the tenderloin lays flat when opened.

2. Season inside with salt, pepper and dried sage. Lay 2 sage leaves on one side of each tenderloin and fold over. Wrap 1 slice of bacon around each tenderloin.

3. Preheat 12" skillet on medium high heat. Add duck fat or butter. Brown turkey for 8 minutes on each side. Pour in white wine and cover quickly. Reduce heat to low and simmer for 15 minutes, or until turkey is cooked through. Remove turkey and keep warm.

4. Raise heat to medium high. Simmer pan juices while stirring until reduced and thickened. Serve turkey sliced with pan juices on top.

Options:
SCD & Paleo:
Use dairy-free butter.

Note:
I like to make a stew with the leftovers. I chop the pork into bitesized pieces, add cooked peas and carrots, and additional broth. If you can tolerate cream, it's a wonderful addition.

PORK TENDERLOIN WITH DILL SAUCE

I like to make this just to have the delicious leftovers.

2 pork tenderloins
1 Tbs olive oil
2 shallots sliced
1 Tbs butter or substitute
2 Tbs chopped fresh dill

1/4 cup white wine
1/4 cup chicken broth or water
1 Tbs Dijon mustard
1/4 tsp herbed sea salt
1/4 tsp freshly ground pepper

1. Preheat oven to 350° F. Have a heat-proof glass baking dish ready that is just large enough for the fillets.

2. Preheat 12" skillet on medium high heat. Add olive oil, and swirl to coat the pan. Add pork tenderloins and season with herbed sea salt and pepper. Cook tenderloins about 7 minutes per side or until lightly browned.

3. Turn off heat. Remove tenderloins and place in prepared baking dish. Put skillet aside for when preparing sauce. Place tenderloins in preheated oven and roast uncovered for 15 minutes, or until internal temperature reads 160° F.

4. Meanwhile place butter in pan and return to medium heat. Saute shallots in butter for 5 minutes. Add dill, white wine, broth, and mustard. Simmer until reduced to a thick sauce, approximately 10 minutes. Adjust seasonings if needed.

5. Slice tenderloin and serve with dill and mustard sauce.

SCD
GF
Nut-Free
DF option

Options:

* Look for prosciutto without sugar. Good prosciutto should only contain pork and salt.

** Look for roasted artichokes in olive oil. I use Seggiano's roasted artichokes and tapenade.

Notes:

This can be rather salty due to the prosciutto and capers. If you are trying to reduce your salt intake, omit the prosciutto and capers.

Lentil pasta is very high in nickel. Eat it sparingly if you have a nickel allergy.

Lentil Pasta with Roasted Artichokes

Bean pasta is a great substitute for grain pasta, and it is very nutricious.

8 oz. box of lentil pasta
2 Tbs olive oil divided
1 large onion sliced
1/2 cup roasted artichokes**
1-23 oz jar of tomato sauce

4 slices prosciutto* (optional)
4 Tbs artichoke tapenade**
1 Tbs capers drained
1/2 tsp salt
fresh basil for garnish

1. Fill large pot with water. Bring to a simmer until ready to cook pasta.

2. In a 12" skillet, heat 1 Tbs olive oil over medium-high heat. Add onion and saute 5 minutes.

3. Slice artichokes into bite-sized pieces and add to skillet along with tomato sauce. Bring to a simmer. Cook for 5 minutes.

4. Chop prosciutto into bite-sized pieces and add to sauce if using. Turn off heat.

5. Meanwhile bring water in large pot to boil over high heat and add salt. Pour in pasta and stir until water returns to boiling. Cover pot, reduce heat to low boil, and cook for 7-9 minutes. Keep an eye on the pot, as it tends to create a lot of foam. When al dente, drain in colander and rinse with cold water.

6. Toss pasta with additional 1 Tbs olive oil and sauce. Serve garnished with artichoke tapenade, capers, and basil.

Options:
*SCD & Paleo:
Use dairy-free butter.

*When using fresh plum tomatoes, peel and seed to reduce inflammation. Add a bit of water or white wine to aid in cooking.

If you can tolerate dairy, this dish traditionally has 1/2 cup sour cream added at the end.

Tomato & Turkey Paprikash

This dish made me into a smoked paprika lover.

1 lb. turkey fillets cut in bite-sized pieces
1 large red onion sliced
1 16 oz. can of diced tomatoes or 5 plum tomatoes diced*
3 Tbs olive oil, divided
1/4 cup turkey or chicken broth
2 Tbs smoked paprika
1/4 cup fresh chopped dill or 2 Tbs dried
salt and pepper to taste

1. Heat 1 Tbs olive oil in 12" skillet on medium high heat. Add turkey, season with salt and pepper, and saute until just cooked through, approximately 8 to 10 minutes. Lower heat to medium and remove turkey from pan and keep warm.

2. Add the remaining 2 Tbs olive oil to the same skillet and add onion. Saute until translucent and lightly browned. Add paprika and toss to coat onions. Add tomatoes and continue cooking until they begin to breakdown.

3. Add reserved turkey (along with any accumulated juices), broth and dill and simmer until thickened. Serve garnished with dill.

QUICHE

Quiche Base

4 eggs
1/2 tsp herbed sea salt

1 cup half-and-half or substitute⁎
1/4 tsp pepper

Whisk together and put aside.

Savory Pastry Crust

1/3 cup coconut flour
1/4 cup golden flax meal
1/2 tsp salt

1 Tbs chia seeds
1/3 cup butter or substitute⁎
1 Tbs (or more) cold water

Preheat oven to 350° F. Place all dry ingredients in a bowl and mix. Using a pastry blender or forks, mix in butter, and add just enough cold water for crust to come together. Press crust into a 9" or 10" quiche pan or pie plate. Prebake crust at 350° F for 10 minutes. Remove from oven and allow to cool briefly.

Non-Dairy Fillings

1 large tomato sliced thin (drain on paper towel for 5 minutes)
1 Tbs scallions sliced thin
2 to 3 Tbs pesto swirled through the quiche base

1 cup asparagus cut into small pieces and blanched for 3 minutes
1/4 cup sugar-free smoked salmon chopped
2 tsp fresh dill or 1 tsp dried

Cheese Fillings

1 cup fresh spinach, chopped fine
1 cup Swiss cheese grated
1 Tbs scallions (white and green parts) sliced thin

1 cup roasted butternut squash or pumpkin
1/2 cup arugula or kale, chopped and steamed briefly
1 cup feta cheese crumbled

1/2 cup broccoli florettes, chopped and blanched for 3 minutes.
2 slices sugar-free bacon, cooked until crisp and crumbled
1 cup cheddar cheese, grated
1 Tbs chives, snipped, and 1 tsp sage leaves, minced

1. Place filling ingredients in prepared crust, pour quiche base over, and top with cheese (if using) and bake at 350° F for 20 to 30 minutes, or until just set and puffed. Serve warm or at room temperature. Refrigerate any leftovers.

SCD option
Paleo option
GF
Nut-Free
DF option

Options:
⁎**SCD & Paleo:**
Use dairy-free butter, and cream and omit cheeses.

Note:
These can also be made in 12 greased muffin cups. Prebake crust for 5 minutes. After adding filling, reduce cooking time to 10 to 15 minutes or until just set.

SCD
Paleo
GF
Nut-Free
DF

Options:

*SCD & Paleo:
Use chicken stock in
place of white wine.
Use dairy-free butter.

CHICKEN & MUSHROOM PICCATA

2 large skinless, boneless, chicken breasts sliced in half lengthwise
1 small egg beaten
salt and pepper to taste
2 Tbs butter, divided
2 shallots sliced
6 mushrooms sliced

3 garlic cloves sliced
1 Tbs capers plus 1 tsp brine
1/3 cup white wine or stock*
3 sprigs parsley leaves

1. In a small bowl whisk together egg, salt, and pepper. Put aside.

2. Dip each chicken cutlet into egg mixture. Heat 1 Tbs butter in 12" skillet on medium-high heat and brown cutlet in butter, turning until just cooked through, approximately 8 to 10 minutes. Remove cutlets from pan and keep warm.

3. In the same skillet add the remaining 1 Tbs butter. Lower heat to medium, and add garlic and shallots. Saute until translucent, then add mushrooms and continue sauteing until lightly browned.

4. Add capers and caper juice, white wine and 2 sprigs of parsley and bring to a simmer. Stir occationally until liquid is reduced and thickened.

5. Slice cooked chicken cutlets and serve with mushroom sauce and garnish with remaining 1 sprig fresh parsely leaves.

Venison Oven Roast

Paleo
GF
Nut-Free
DF
Low Nickel

Options:
If you don't have venison, you can make this with a pork roast, beef top round or butt roast.

Marinade: Whisk together and put aside.

1/4 cup olive oil	3 garlic cloves, minced
2 Tbs red wine vinegar	1 Tbs Dijon mustard
1/2 tsp dried thyme	1/4 tsp pepper

Venison Roast:

3 lb. venison roast	2 Tbs duck fat
1/2 tsp salt	2 onions chopped
1 cup chicken or beef broth	1/4 cup red wine
1 bay leaf	2 tsp Dijon mustard

1. Place venison roast in a covered glass dish. Coat well with marinade on all sides. Cover and refrigerate for 2 to 3 days, turnings twice a day, and spooning marinade over the top.

2. Preheat over to 350° F. Heat large Dutch oven over medium-high heat, add duck fat, and onions and saute for 5 minutes. Remove onions and reserve.

3. Remove venison roast from marinade. Discard marinade. Sprinkle venison with salt. In the same dutch oven, over medium high heat, sear the venison roast on all sides. Turn off heat. Add broth, red wine, and bay leaf.

4. Cover Dutch oven and place in preheated 350° F oven. Roast for 1 hour. Add the reserved onions, cover, and continue roasting for another 1/2 hour to 1 hour, or until very tender, and interior temperature reaches 160° F.

5. Remove pot from oven and place on stove top. Place venison roast on a deep plate to rest. Meanwhile bring pan juices to a simmer, add remaining 2 tsp Dijon mustard, and de-glaze pan by scraping and stirring pan juices. Simmer, stirring occasionally, until thickened. Pour through a stainer before serving.

6. Slice venison roast thinly, and serve with pan gravy.

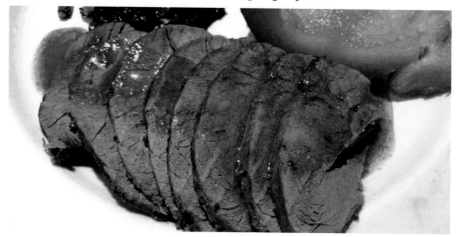

Broccoli Rabe Pasta

There is something addictive about the bitter, nuttiness of broccoli rabe. My Italian grandmother Noni made a version of this for me many times.

1 1/2 cups fresh broccoli rabe, chopped (leaves, stems & flowers)
2 garlic cloves, sliced   1/2 Tbs capers, with juice
1 small onion, sliced   5 slices of prosciutto, chopped
1 1/2 Tbs olive oil   3/4 cup broth
2 Tbs parsley, chopped   salt and pepper to taste
1-8 oz. box green lentil pasta   1tsp salt for pasta water

Topping*
1 Tbs salted butter or substitute   1 small garlic clove, minced
1 Tbs olive oil   1/3 cup golden flax meal

1. Fill a large pasta pot with water, and heat over medium heat until ready to cook pasta. Make the topping by sauteing garlic in butter and olive oil over medium heat for 1 minute. Add golden flax meal and continue stirring until all oils have been absorbed and mixture is crisp and crumbly. Put aside.

2. In a large saute pan heat 1 Tbs olive oil on medium high heat, and add garlic and onions. Saute until translucent, then add broccoli rabe and continue sauteing for 2 minutes or until just wilted. Add prosciutto and broth, reduce heat to low, cover, and simmer for 5 minutes.

3. Bring pasta water to a boil and add 1 tsp salt. Stir in pasta, reduce heat to medium high, and simmer for 7 minutes, or follow package directions.

4. While pasta is simmering, uncover broccoli rabe, and raise heat to medium high and continue simmering until liquid is reduced and thickened. Turn off heat.

5. When pasta is done, drain, and add to broccoli rabe mixture. Add capers, 1 Tbs parsley and 1 Tbs of the topping. Toss to coat. Taste and adjust seasonings.

6. Serve hot, topped with remaining parsley and garlic-flax topping.

Options:

*If you are a fan of anchovies, add 3 to the topping when sauting the garlic.

Notes:
Lentil pasta is very high in nickel. Eat it sparingly if you have a nickel allergy.

MEMORABLE *Desserts*

Some of us live for dessert. We patiently get through a delicious meal, with our sights set on the sweet finale. After nearly every meal, I hear Frederick utter the same line, "So is there any dessert in our future?" Even though I no longer bake with grains, sugars or dairy, he still looks forward to dessert. I guess I'm doing something right.

My mother has been making apple pies worthy of a blue ribbon my entire life. She taught me her tricks as soon as I was able to stand on a chair and peek over the counter. These pies are still sought after by friends and family. When a notable chef requested her pies each time he visited, I knew it wasn't just my childhood imaginings. These were truly something special. Pie making teaches you many important lessons: you learn about temperature, the butter must be chilled, and water icy. The flour should not be fine, but gritty. The apples should be ripe and fragrant and preferably Macintosh. When you cut and roll the pastry crust, do it with an economy of strokes. Flip the pastry deftly off the roller and into the pie plate, arrange apples tightly in a spiral, dot with butter, cover with the top crust, and brush lightly with milk. Sprinkle with sugar and cut a pattern in the top. All of these steps taught me how to pay attention to the methods, as much as the materials. How many apple pies has my mother made? Probably hundreds, but practice makes perfect.

My mother and grandmother also made chocolate icebox cakes. When I first had this frozen treat, I thought it would be hard to make. When they showed me how to layer whipped cream with cookies and put it into the freezer, I was stunned at it's simplicity. Later on I realized how just a few good ingredients can make something memorable. I enjoyed a slice of ripe melon wrapped with a paper thin piece of lean prosciutto as an end course at a restaurant near the Vatican. A perfectly ripe peach half only needs a dusting of freshly grated nutmeg. A fabulous ice cream can be made with chocolate mint leaves steeped in half and half, and mixed with a touch of honey. Find what is at it's peak, and prepare it simply.

As a child, I remember my father bringing home French pastries from a bakery in Chester, CT, near his office. My first croissant was a landmark experience. Then there was the first chocolate croissant...sigh. But the pastry that really impressed me was the coffee daquoise. These round pastries had crispy hazelnut meringues layered with coffee buttercream, and topped with a dusting of cocoa and a toasted hazelnut. I hadn't tasted a hazelnut before this, but to be presented with this gustatorial delight was life changing. I marveled at the contrasting textures, the elegant buttercream, and complex flavors.

 My grandparents, Noni and Nono, brought us Italian pastries when they visited from

New York. The flavors of these pastries were yet another new experience. They were not sweet, and many were quite chewy, but the flavors of orange, amaretto, anise, and rum were delightful. My favorite part was the custard filling in the cannollis; it was silky smooth and so satisfying. I also loved the rum cakes which were a glossy brown on the outside and light, airy, and moist on the inside.

I recognized the same flavors at the gelato bars I visited on my travels through Italy. Each establishment had the common vanilla, chocolate, and coffee gelato, but then they diversified into various fruits, nuts, liqueurs, and spices. I adored the banana gelato, craved the hazelnut gelato, but the one that I will never forget was the "Zuppa Inglese" or English Soup. It was made at a small gelato bar in Firenze, and included all the ingredients found in an English trifle. Talk about cross-culture food! I later experienced the Italian version of the trifle called tiramisu, which translates to "pick me up" or "cheer me up". This may have something to do with its generous dose of espresso, but its layers of sponge cake, marscarpone, and cocoa powder are bound to make one happy. Now that I don't eat some of these delicacies, I find I'm just as content with my version of bread pudding.

I have always found unusual flavors and ingredients an inspiring challenge. Noni made fried squash flowers that she dusted with powdered sugar and grated Parmesan. These were technically not a dessert, but she taught me to look at food not as a category, but as unique combinations of ingredients. A pine nut can be a very different thing depending on if it's topping ricotta pie or mixed with basil in pesto. My friend Jan Hall gave me one of her mother's recipes for basil cake. It used dried basil in a pound cake base. The basil added a wonderful liquorice flavor.

My mother and I used to visit herb folklorist Adelma Simmons at Caprilands, in Coventry CT. I was surprised, at first, to find a recipe for chocolate sauerkraut cake in one of her cook books. After tasting a piece, it became one of my favorite chocolate cakes. Adelma would also place rose geranium leaves at the bottom of a cake pan, and pour an unflavored pound cake batter on top. The leaves would be removed before serving, but infused the cake with a delicate flavor.

This inspired me to create a multi tiered rose geranium cake for out wedding. Adelma's recipe turned out to be much too sweet for my taste, but I still use rose geranium leaves to flavor my grain free cakes when the occasion calls for something special.

These unique combinations gave me the courage to explore alternative ingredients. When I develop a new dessert, sometimes I modify one of my old favorites; but I try to let the creation take on it's own character. Do I miss the foods I can no longer eat? Yes, and no. But I'm grateful for the memories and the lessons.

96

Desserts & Snacks

DRIED FRUIT BROWNIES

Paleo option
GF
Nut-Free
Spice-free
DF option

Options:
Experiment with various dried fruits in these brownies:

- figs
- apricots
- dried cherries

Paleo option:
Use dairy-free butter.

You may substitute almond flour for the sunflower meal.

Notes:
*If using unsalted butter, increase salt to 1/2 tsp.

Sunflower meal, some dried fruits, and cocoa are very high in nickel. Eat them sparingly if you have a nickel allergy.

Prepare yourself . . . you may be making one batch after another of these brownies. They have the added bonus of tasting just as fabulous when substituting cocoa powder for the carob powder if you can tolerate chocolate. You can also use a variety of dried fruits as the base.

1 cup chopped dates soaked in 2 Tbs rum, fruit juice or water
3/4 cup butter or substitute*   1/2 cup golden flax meal
1/2 cup honey   1/2 cup coconut flour
3 large eggs   1 cup sunflower meal *(pg. 150)*
3/4 cups carob or cocoa powder   1/2 tsp baking soda
1/4 tsp sea salt

1. Preheat oven to 350° F. Place butter and honey in a mixer and combine. Add eggs and mix well. Add soaked dried fruit and dry ingredients and mix well. If dough is too stiff, add up to 1/4 cup of additional water or fruit juice.

2. Spread batter evenly in an 8" or 9" silicone baking pan or greased pan.

3. Bake for 20 minutes for fudgy brownies, or 30 minutes for cake brownies.

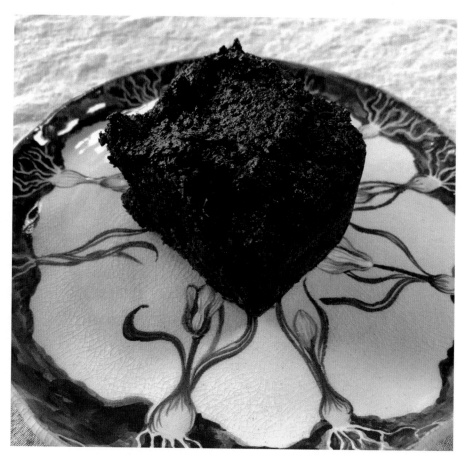

SCD option
Paleo option
GF
Nut-Free
DF option

Options:
SCD & Paleo:
Substitute almond flour for flax meal, and dairy-free cream and yogurt.

Notes:
* Pumpkin Puree: Place whole pumpkin in glass or ceramic baking dish. Poke 3 holes in the top with knife, and roast in preheated 350°F oven for 45 minutes, or until very soft. When cool, cut in half, remove seeds and skin, and puree. Drain excess liquid using a fine stainer. *Or use plain canned pumpkin.*

Serving Suggestions:
Mix 1 cup of plain yogurt with 1 Tbs honey. Serve as a topping for each slice with a dusting of grated nutmeg.

PUMPKIN PIE

Dust Crust

1 Tbs golden flax meal
1 Tbs coconut flour
1/2 Tbs butter or substitute

1 tsp date sugar
1/4 tsp sea salt

1. Coat the bottom and sides of a 9" pie plate with butter. In a small bowl combine flax meal, coconut flour, date sugar and salt. Dust the entire buttered surface of the pie plate, tilting and shaking to coat. Put aside.

Filling

1 1/4 cups pumpkin puree*
1 1/4 cup cream or substitute
1/2 cup honey
6 eggs
1 tsp date sugar (optional)

1/8 tsp ground fenugreek
1 tsp cinnamon
1/2 tsp nutmeg
1/2 tsp ground cloves
1 Tbs rum or vanilla

1. In a large bowl combine filling ingredients with a whisk. Pour into prepared pie plate

2. Bake at 375° F for 40 to 50 minutes or until edges are set and center is just a bit jiggly. Turn off oven and leave pie with door cracked open, for another 10 minutes. Serve warm or chilled. Refrigerate leftovers.

SUNFLOWER & RASPBERRY LINZER BARS

Options:

*Paleo option:
Use dairy-free butter.

You can substitute strawberry or apricot fruit spread for the raspberry spread.

SCD option:
Use dairy-free butter. Substitute almond flour for sunflower meal, increase to 1 1/2 cups, and omit flax meal.

Notes:

Bake long enough for the fruit filling to start bubbling and thicken but not so long that the dough gets dry.

Sunflower meal and raspberries are very high in nickel. Eat them sparingly if you have a nickel allergy.

These are simply wonderful, and very close to the original.

1/2 cup butter or substitute*   1 cup sunflower meal *(p. 150)*
1/3 cup honey   1/2 tsp cinnamon
1 1/2 Tbs date sugar   1/4 tsp ground cloves
4 eggs   1/4 tsp sea salt
1/2 cup golden flax meal   3/4 cup raspberry fruit spread
1/2 cup coconut flour

1. Preheat oven to 325° F. Cream together butter, honey, and date sugar. Add eggs and mix until light and fluffy.

2. Add dry ingredients and blend together. Spread 2/3 of the batter on the bottom of an 8" or 9" square baking pan. Spread the raspberry fruit spread evenly on top of the batter.

3. With wet hands make coils with the remaining dough and create a lattice on top of the fruit.

4. Bake for 25 to 30 minutes or until filling is bubbling and crust is lightly brown.

CHERRY CHOCOLATE CHIP COOKIES

Paleo option
GF
Nut-Free
DF option

Options:

*Paleo option:
Use dairy-free butter.

You can substitute dried cranberries and orange rind for the cherries and vanilla.

Raisins and cinnamon or dried apricots also go nicely with chocolate chips.

Notes:

*If using unsalted butter, increase salt to 1/2 tsp.

Sunflower meal and chocolate are very high in nickel. Eat them sparingly if you have a nickel allergy.

Don't make these assuming they'll be like Tole House chocolate chip cookies. They're darn good as they are though.

1 1/2 cup sunflower meal *(p. 150)*
1/4 cup golden flax meal
1/4 cup coconut flour
2 Tbs date sugar
1/8 tsp sea salt
1/2 tsp baking soda

1/3 cup butter or substitute*
1/4 cup honey
1 egg
1/2 cup dried cherries
1/2 tsp vanilla
1/3 cup chocolate chips

1. Preheat oven to 350° F. Cream together butter, honey, and egg. Add dry ingredients and mix well. Add dried cherries, vanilla, and chocolate chips.

2. Drop balls of dough on parchment lined cookie sheets, and press lightly to flatten. Bake for 10 to 12 minutes.

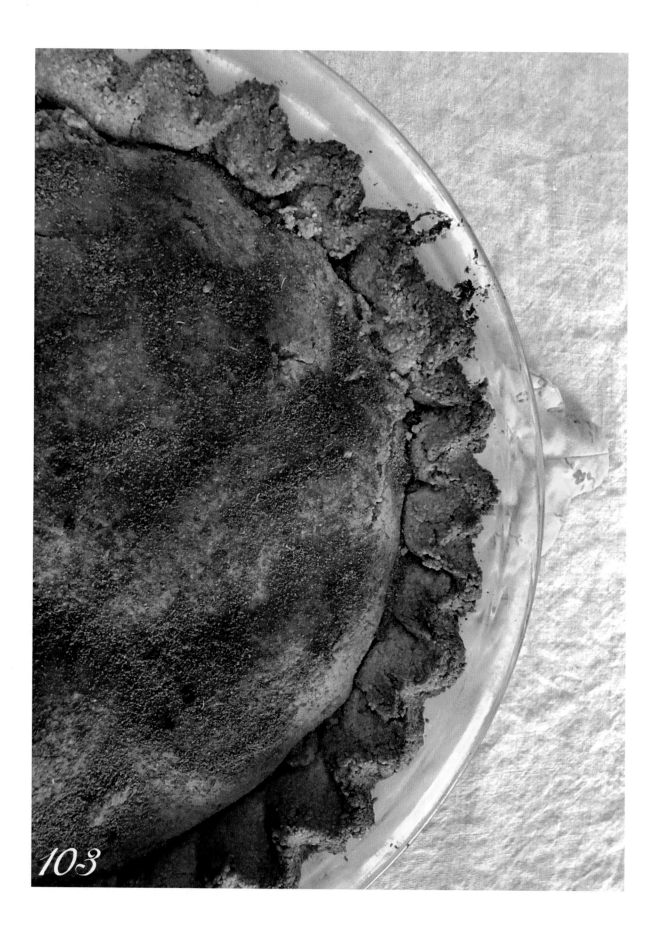

103

APPLE PIE

Apple Pie is one of my all-time favorite desserts. It took four years for me to find the combination of light crispy crust and thick rich filling that makes it so satisfying. Because the filling for this pie doesn't have any thickeners, a bottom crust would get too soggy. That is why this pie only has a top crust.

Pie Crust

1 cup sunflower meal *(p. 150)*

1/4 cup golden flax meal

1/3 cup coconut flour

1/3 cup duck fat, or butter*

1/4 tsp sea salt

3 to 4 Tbs ice water

1. In a food processor, combine sunflower meal, flax meal, coconut, and salt. Blend, then add duck fat and pulse until coarse lumps form. Add ice water, 1 Tbs at a time until dough just comes together.

2. Form dough into a circle and place off-center on a of piece of waxed paper or parchment 24" long. Fold in half so dough is in the center. With a rolling pin, form a 9 1/2" to 10" circle. Fold edges of paper over and place on cookie sheet in freezer for 1 hour or over night. Keep frozen until ready to bake.

Filling

7 to 8 cooking apples, peeled and sliced (mixed varieties)

6 Tbs butter or butter substitute*

1/2 cup honey

3/4 tsp cinnamon

1/2 tsp nutmeg

1/4 tsp ground cloves

1 tsp date sugar for top

1. Preheat oven to 375°F. Place large (at least 10"x 10") cutting board in freezer.

2. In a 12" skillet heat butter and honey. Add sliced apples and turn heat up to medium high. Saute, stirring until apples are golden brown and honey butter is caramelized (about 10 to 15 minutes). Place apples into 9" glass pie plate and sprinkle top with spices. Allow to cool for at least 15 minutes.

3. Remove pie crust packet with cookie sheet and cutting board from freezer and place on cool counter. Unfold edges of waxed paper and remove top sheet. Sprinkle surface of crust lightly with coconut flour using a sifter.

4. Place cooled cutting board on top of crust and cookie sheet. Placing one hand on each side. Flip these over so the cutting board is on the bottom. Remove cookie sheet. Place cutting board with crust above apple filling and slide the cutting board away while fitting crust on top of filling. Remove remaining waxed paper.**

5. Form decorative crust edge by alternating one index finger pressed against thumb and index finger of opposite hand, and sprinkle with date sugar.

4. Bake at 375° F for 20 to 30 minutes or until top crust is golden. Best served immediately, while still warm.

Options:

*Paleo option:
Use dairy-free butter.

*SCD option:
Substitute almond flour for sunflower meal, and omit flax meal. Use dairy-free butter.

• You can add 1 cup fresh cranberries for an autumn treat.

• Dried apricots and raisins are another nice addition.

Note:

**Transferring Crust on to filling can be tricky. If you end up with pieces, no worries. Patch it up and it will still be delicious!

Sunflower meal is very high in nickel. Eat it sparingly if you have a nickel allergy.

Coconut Cakes with Mango

SCD
Paleo
GF
Nut-Free
Spice-Free
DF option

Options:

＊ If you can't find the dried mango or coconut flavoring, replace coconut flavoring with 1/2 tsp each of nutmeg and cinnamon and a dash of ground cloves. Serve with warm applesauce.

Notes:

Coconut is very high in nickel. Avoid this recipe if you have a nickel allergy.

If you don't have mini bundt pans, these can be made in a muffin or cake pan. If you can't find dried mango, use apple sauce. See sidebar.

Mango Puree＊＊
Pour 1/4 cup boiling water over 3 pieces of dried mango. Soak until soft (1 hr.), then puree with 1 Tbs of liquid till smooth.

Cakes

4 Tbs coconut oil	1/2 cup coconut flour
1/2 cup honey	1/4 cup toasted unsweetened coconut
4 eggs	1/2 tsp coconut flavoring＊
1/4 tsp sea salt	toasted unsweetened coconut for garnish

1. Preheat oven to 350° F. Cream together coconut oil and honey. Add eggs and remaining ingredients. Mix, scraping down sides, until light and fluffy.

2. Divide batter between 6 silicone mini bundt cups. For support, place silicone on baking sheet, and bake for 20 to 25 minutes, or until puffed and just barely set. Cool slightly, remove from silicone cups, and serve with mango puree and toasted coconut.

**Paleo option
GF
Nut-Free
DF option**

Options:

***Paleo option:**
Use dairy-free butter,
and toppings.

**Other Fruit
Combos:**
• Strawberry &
rhubarb
• Peach & blueberry
• Apple & craneberry
• Plum & ginger
• Mango, banana &
pinapple

Note:
*If using unsalted
butter, increase salt
to 1/2 tsp.

Serve with:
• Whipped cream
• Honey sweetened
ice cream
• Coconut yogurt
mixed with honey

FRUIT CRUMBLE

There are endless options for fruit filling, but I'll share one of my favorites.

Topping
1/2 cup sunflower meal *(pg. 150)*
1/2 cup coconut flour
1/4 cup golden flax meal
2 Tbs date sugar
1/4 tsp sea salt
1/2 cup butter or substitute*
1 Tbs honey
1/2 tsp nutmeg or cinnamon

Fruit Filling
1 pint fresh blueberries
1 quart fresh strawberries
1/3 cup honey

1. Preheat oven to 350° F. Mix together topping ingredients with a pastry blender or food processor. Put aside.

2. Rinse fruit and cut strawberries into quarters. In an 8" or 9" square baking dish, mix together fruit and drizzle with honey. Crumble topping evenly over fruit.

3. Bake for 25 to 30 minutes or until filling is bubbling. Serve warm on it's own or with optional toppings.

Banana Carob Bread

**Paleo option
GF
Nut-Free
DF option**

Banana, cardamom and carob make such nice companions.

Options:

*Paleo option:
Use dairy-free butter.

If you don't care for carob, substitute coco or unsweetened coconut flakes.

Note:

*If using unsalted butter, increase salt to 1/2 tsp.

Carob and dates are moderately high in nickel. Use in moderation if you have a nickel allergy.

1/3 cup dates, pitted, chopped, & soaked in 1 Tbs rum or water
1 ripe banana
1/2 cup coconut flour
1/4 cup golden flax meal
1/4 cup carob powder
4 large eggs
1/3 cup butter or substitute*

1/4 cup honey
1/2 tsp baking soda
1/4 tsp sea salt
1/4 tsp cinnamon
1/4 tsp cardamom

1. Preheat oven to 350° F.

2. Place banana, coconut flour, flaxmeal, and carob in a mixer or large bowl and blend. Add eggs and mix well. Add butter and honey and mix until light and fluffy. Add baking soda, salt, spices, and dates and mix briefly.

3. Pour batter into a buttered loaf pan and bake for 30 to 35 minutes, or until set. Let cool before slicing.

SIMPLE CHOCOLATE CAKE

For birthdays, special occasions, and "just because" days.

Cake Batter

5 eggs & 1 white *(reserve 1 yolk)*
1/4 cup golden flax meal
1/2 cup butter or substitute*
1/2 cup honey
1/2 cup coconut flour

1/2 cup cocoa or carob powder
1 tsp baking soda
1/2 cup boiling water
1/4 tsp salt
1 tsp flavoring of choice**

1. Preheat oven to 350° F. Grease the inside of two 8" round cake pans. Place a circle of parchment on the bottom of each pan.

2. Combine eggs and flax meal in the bowl of a mixer. Add butter and honey and combine. Add cocoa and coconut flour, baking soda, and salt. Beat at high speed for 3 minutes. Reduce to low speed and slowly add boiling water. Add flavoring at the end and blend briefly.

3. Divide batter between two prepared cake pans. Bake for 20 to 25 minutes. Cake is done when puffed and a tooth pick inserted in the center comes out clean. Allow cakes to cool before removing from pans and peeling off parchment.

Chocolate Butter Cream Frosting

1 cup butter or substitute, softened
1/2 cup coconut oil, softened
1/2 cup honey

1 egg yolk
1/2 cup cocoa or carob powder

1. Place all frosting ingredients in a mixer with whisk attachment and blend. Stop and scrape down the sides with a rubber spatula. If mixture is too liquid, refrigerate for 10 to 15 minutes. Return to the mixer and continue whisking at high speed until light and thick. Refrigerate until ready to use. Remove from the refrigerator 15 minutes before spreading.

To serve: Place one cake layer on a dessert plate. Spread top with a 1/4" layer of frosting and top with second cake layer. Decorate with remaining frosting. Serve immediately or refrigerate until ready to serve.

**Paleo option
GF
Nut-Free
DF option**

Options:
*Paleo option:
Use dairy-free butter.

**Use your favorite flavoring:
• Vanilla
• Mint
• Orange
• Rum

Note:
*If using unsalted butter, increase salt to 1/2 tsp.

These can also be made as 12 cupcakes. Reduce baking time to 15 to 20 minutes.

Cocoa and chocolate are very high in nickel. Use sparingly if you have a nickel allergy. Carob is only moderately high in nickel, making it a good substitute.

Anise Cakes

SCD option
Paleo option
GF
Nut-Free
DF option

Options:

Paleo option:
Use dairy-free butter.

SCD option:
Use dairy-free butter.
Substitute almond
flour for flax meal.

Note:

*If using unsalted
butter, increase salt
to 1/2 tsp.

You may have left-
over cinnamon date
sugar. This can be
used on top of scones
or muffins before
baking, or stored
for future use in an
airtight container.

I was introduced to these little cakes at Caprilands Herb Farm. The proprietress, Adelma Simmons was sometimes called a "witch," which she never denied. They do seem to hold magical properties. Many times my mother and I would find we made these cookies on the same day while hundreds of miles apart. In Italy, where anise has been revered for centuries as a digestive, they were enjoyed at the end of wedding feasts.

Batter

1/2 cup butter or substitute*	2 eggs
1/3 cup honey	1/2 cup coconut flour
1/4 cup golden flax meal	1/4 tsp sea salt
1 Tbs whole anise seed	

Cinnamon and date sugar coating

2 tsp cinnamon	1 1/2 Tbs date sugar, sifted

1. Preheat oven to 350° F. Line a sheet pan with parchment paper.

2. Place butter and honey in mixer and blend together. Mix in flax meal, and anise seed, and then add eggs. Beat for 1 minute, then add coconut flour, and salt and mix well. Let sit for a few minutes to thicken.

3. In a small, deep bowl mix together cinnamon and date sugar. Using a cookie scoop or spoon, place balls of dough one at a time in mixture. Swirl each ball of batter around until well coated, then place 2" apart on prepared sheet pan.

4. Bake for 12 to 15 minutes, or until just puffed and slight cracks appear on top. Let cool briefly before removing to serving dish.

Sunflower Apricot Bars

With sunflower butter and coconut, these bars really stick to your ribs and keep you going. Because they do not have eggs or butter, they also travel well.

2 Tbs chia seeds

1 Tbs flax meal

1/2 cup apple juice or water

1/4 cup coconut flour

3/4 cup unsweetened, shredded coconut

1/2 cup dried apricots, diced

1/4 tsp salt

2 Tbs honey

3/4 cup sunflower butter

1. Preheat oven to 350° F. Mix together chia seeds, flax meal, and water. Put aside.

2. Mix together coconut flour, coconut, and salt. Put aside.

3. In a mixer or bowl, blend together sunflower butter and honey. Add dry ingredients and blend. Add chia mixture and apricots. Mix well into a stiff dough.

4. Spread dough evenly in an 8"x 8" baking dish. Using a spatula or knife score into 9 or 12 bars.

5. Bake for 20 to 25 minutes, or until very lightly browned.

6. Allow to cool for 10 minutes before dividing into bars. Store in an airtight container for up to 1 week.

Paleo
GF
Nut-Free
DF
Spice-Free
Egg-Free
Vegetarian

Options:

Substitute peanut butter for the sunbutter if you can eat nuts.

Substitute raisins dried mango, or dried cherries for the dried apricots.

Notes:

Sunflower butter and apricots are very high in nickel. Eat them sparingly if you have a nickel allergy.

LEMON BALM SHORTBREAD

Fresh lemon balm provides a welcome flavor to baked goods when you have a citrus allergy. It gives this shortbread a bright zing which pairs well with most fresh fruit. It is also delicious topped with fruit sweetened jams.

1 cup sunflower meal *(pg. 150)*   1/2 cup butter or substitute*
1/4 cup flax meal   3 Tbs honey
2 Tbs date sugar   2 Tbs lemon balm leaves, shredded**
1/2 cup coconut flour   1/2 tsp salt

1. Preheat oven to 350° F.

2. Place dry ingredients in a bowl. Blend with a pastry blender. Add butter, honey, and lemon balm leaves and blend together.

3. Spread evenly in 8"x 8" baking pan, and score into 9 pieces with a knife or spatula.

4. Bake for 20 to 25 minutes or until lightly brown and crisp. Cool before removing from pan.

Options:

*If using unsalted butter, increase salt to 3/4 tsp.

Paleo option:
*Use dairy-free butter.

SCD option:
*Use dairy-free butter. Substitute almond flour for sunflower meal and omit flax meal and increase coconut flour by 1/4 cup.

** Use fresh mint, lavender, or dried basil in place of the lemon balm.

Note:
Sunflower seeds are very high in nickel. Eat them sparingly if you have a nickel allergy.

**Paleo option
GF
Nut-Free
DF option
Low Nickel**

Options:

Low Nickel:
Use dairy half-and-half

Paleo:
Use non-dairy creamer

❋ Coconut creamer makes a good substitute for half and half. Nut milk will work, but the consistency may not be as firm.

BAKED CUSTARD

3 cups half-and-half or substitute❋
5 large eggs
1/2 cup honey

1 tsp vanilla
1/4 tsp sea salt
1/2 tsp nutmeg, divided

1. Preheat oven to 325 ° F. Place 6 to 8 custard cups in a 2" deep baking pan. Boil 2-3 cups of water and keep warm. Put aside.

2. Scald half and half (or substitute) in a sauce pan on medium high heat until steaming. Turn off heat, and leave half and half in pan.

3. In a large bowl whisk together eggs and honey. Pour 1 cup of hot half and half slowly into egg mixture while whisking constantly to temper eggs. Continue whisking and add remaining half and half. Add vanilla and salt, and divide equally among custard cups inside baking dish. Sprinkle each with nutmeg.

4. Move pan to the front of the middle shelf in preheated oven. Carefully pour boiling water into baking pan around the custard cups to come 1/2 way up their sides. Slide to center of oven.

5. Bake for 30 to 45 minutes, or until set around edges but still jiggly in the center. Can be served warm or chilled. Refrigerate any leftovers.

CAROB & RASPBERRY DACQUOISE

A tempting mix or crunchy cake and creamy filling.

Dacquoise

6 large egg whites, *at room temp.*
1/8 tsp cream of tartar
1/8 tsp sea salt
1/4 cup honey

2 Tbs date sugar
1/2 cup sunflower meal *(pg. 150)*
1/4 cup golden flax meal
1/4 cup of carob or cocoa powder

1. Preheat oven to 300° F. Place parchment on a large sheet pan.

2. Place egg whites, cream of tartar, and salt in the bowl of a mixer. Using the whisk attachment, beat on high speed until soft peaks form. Lower speed and slowly add honey and date sugar. Stop mixer and scrape down sides. Return to high speed and beat until stiff peaks form. Stop mixer.

3. In a small bowl whisk together sunflower meal, flax meal, and carob powder. Add to egg white mixture and blend together with whisk attachment briefly. Using a rubber spatula, scrape down sides to be sure the egg white is incorporated. Do not over mix or egg whites will lose their fluff.

4. Scoop batter onto parchment lined baking sheet in 8 mounds. Spread out into circles approximately 1/2" thick.

4. Bake for 45 minutes to 1 hour, or until set around edges. Turn off oven, and leave door ajar. Let cool before removing from the parchment paper. They should crisp up once they are cool.

Carob Buttercream

1 cup butter or substitute, *softened** 2 egg yolks
1/4 cup honey   1/4 cup of carob or cocoa powder
1/2 tsp. ground cinnamon

1 pint fresh raspberries, or 1/2 cup raspberry fruit preserve*

1. In a mixer combine butter, honey, cinnamon, egg yolks, and carob powder. Using the whisk attachment, blend together. Stop and scrape down the sides with a rubber spatula. Continue whisking at high speed until light and thick. Refrigerate until ready to use.**

To serve: Place one dacquoise on a dessert plate. Coat with a 1/4" layer of buttercream and top with fresh raspberries or fruit preserve. Top with another dacquoise. Add a dollop of buttercream and a raspberry to the top. Repeat with remaining dacquoise. Best served immediately. Store leftovers separately.

Paleo option
GF
Nut-Free
DF option

Options:

*Paleo:
Use dairy-free butter.

Spiced Nut Dacquoise:
Substitute ground hazelnuts or almonds for the sunflower meal. Add 1 tsp. cinnamon and 1/4 tsp. of cloves.

*Substitute fresh strawberries for the raspberries.

Notes:
Be sure to choose a dry day to make dacquoise. Any humidity will make them soggy.

**If the buttercream is too stiff to spread when cold, bring to room temperature. Check frequently until it is spreadable.

CHOCOLATE MINT ICE CREAM

This has been a huge hit with kids, especially if they pick the chocolate mint and help with the prep. I love it for its pure, simple deliciousness.

SCD option
Paleo option
GF
Nut-Free
Spice-Free
Low Nickel
DF option

10 stems of fresh chocolate mint, washed
4 cups half-and-half or non-dairy substitute*
1/3 cup honey

1. Place mint stems in a deep saucepan and cover with half-and-half or milk substitute. Bring to a simmer over medium high heat. Push mint leaves down to be sure they are covered. Once the milk is bubbling, turn the heat off, and let sit for 1 or more hours.

2. Strain out the mint. Add the honey and stir well. Refrigerate for 1 hour.

3. Prepare ice cream maker per manufacturer's instructions.

4. Pour mixture into ice cream maker and follow manufacturer's instructions.

5. Serve with a fresh sprig of chocolate mint.

Options:

***SCD & Paleo:**
Use dairy-free creamer

***Low Nickel:**
Use dairy half-and-half

This herb based ice cream can also be made with lemon balm, rose geranium, thyme, lavender, or other types of mint.

For fruit based ice cream do not heat the mixture. Just add 1 cup of fruit with the honey and proceed with manufacturer's instructions.
Use: blueberries, raspberries, peaches, plums or strawberries.

Note:
* Your ice cream will be creamier if you use whole fat milks.

Banana Coconut Pie

**Paleo
GF
Nut-Free
Spice-Free
DF option**

Options:
* Grass-fed organic gelatin is full of healthy collagen.

** If you can tolerate dairy, you can substitute half-and-half for the coconut milk. Nut milk will work, but the consistency may not be as firm.

Note:
If you don't plan to eat all of the pie in one sitting, you can cut individual slices of plain custard pie, and add topping as you serve them.

Refrigerate any leftovers.

Coconut Dust Crust
2 Tbs coconut
1 Tbs golden flax meal

1 tsp date sugar
1 Tbs butter or substitute

Custard Filling
3 Tbs lukewarm water
1 Tbs unflavored gelatin*
2 1/2 cups coconut milk**
1/4 tsp sea salt
2-3 ripe bananas sliced

3 large eggs beaten
1/2 cup honey
1 tsp vanilla or banana flavor
1/2 cup toasted unsweetened coconut
date syrup *(p. 142)*

1. Coat the bottom of a 9" glass pie plate with butter. Combine remaining crust ingredients and dust the bottom and sides of the pie plate. Put aside.

2. In a small bowl combine water and gelatin. Let sit for 10 minutes. Meanwhile, in a large sauce pan heat coconut milk and salt until steaming. Slowly add 1/2 cup of hot coconut milk mixture to beaten eggs, whisking continuously. Add the egg mixture back into the coconut milk in the sauce pan while stirring.

3. Continue to cook the custard over medium high heat for 5 minutes, stirring slowly. Lower the heat if it starts to boil.

4. Add the gelatin and water to the custard and continue cooking and stirring for another 2 to 3 minutes or until completely dissolved. Remove from the heat and add the honey and flavoring. Stir well. Cool for 15 minutes, then pour slowly into prepared pie plate. Refrigerate for 6 hours, or until set.

5. Serve topped with sliced banana, date syrup, and toasted coconut.

116

Blanc Mange

SCD option
Paleo option
GF
Nut-Free
Low Nickel
DF option

Options:

＊SCD & Paleo:
Use non-dairy creamer

＊Low Nickel:
Use dairy half-and-half
Omit chocolate sauce

Chocolate Sauce:
Mix 1/2 cup cocoa or
carob powder with 2
Tbs honey and 2 Tbs of
softened butter. Whisk
together until smooth.

**Lemon Balm
Blanc Mange:**
Add 10 sprigs of fresh
lemon balm to the
half-and-half in the
saucepan. Simmer for
10 minutes. Allow to
cool before straining
out the lemon balm and
squeezing out the half-
and-half. Proceed with
the recipe but omit
vanilla.

Fresh fruit, chocolate sauce, or jam make a wonderful topping for this easy but elegant dessert.

1 1/4 Tbs unflavored gelatin powder
4 Tbs of water
3 cups of half-and-half or substitute＊
1/4 to 1/2 cup honey
1 tsp vanilla (optional)

1. Sprinkle gelatin powder over water and let sit for 10 minutes.

2. Place half-and-half in a sauce pan and bring to a simmer over medium heat. Add gelatin mixture. Continue stirring over medium heat for 5 minutes, or until gelatin is completely dissolved. Add honey and stir to incorporate.

3. Pour through a strainer into custard cups. Chill for 4 hours or more.

Serving suggestions
• Fresh blueberries dusted with nutmeg
• Chocolate sauce and sliced bananas with a sprinkle of cinnamon
• Fresh raspberries and slivers of mint leaves
• Other fresh fruit or jam

**Paleo
GF
Nut-Free
DF option**

Options:

This is also good with banana bread. Substitute chopped dried dates for the apples.

Serve with:

A drizzle of cream, date syrup, warm applesauce or creamed honey

BREAD PUDDING

4 eggs
1 Tbs rum *(optional)*
1/2 cup raisins
2 cups of half-and-half or substitute
1 Tbs date sugar plus more for top *(optional)*
1 recipe of sponge cake *(p. 140)* or other baked good
1 1/2 Tbs butter or substitute, divided

1/4 cup honey
1 cup thinly sliced apples, peeled
2 tsp cinnamon

1. In a large bowl whisk together eggs and honey. Add half-and-half, rum, cinnamon, and date sugar. Whisk to combine and put aside.

2. Using 1/2 Tbs butter, grease the bottom and sides of a deep 9" x 9" baking dish. Cut sponge cake into 18 squares. Place 9 pieces of sponge cake on bottom of baking dish, and dot with 1/2 Tbs butter. Place a layer of apples and raisins evenly spaced on top. End with a layer of sponge cake.

3. Pour egg mixture slowly over the sponge cake. Press down gently to keep sponge cake from floating. If needed, add weight on top. Let sit to soak up egg mixture for 30 minutes. Meanwhile, preheat oven to 350° F.

4. Remove weight. Dot evenly with remaining butter and sprinkle the top with additional date sugar. Bake for 30 to 35 minutes or until just set. Slice and serve warm or at room temperature. Refrigerate any leftovers.

HERB BISCUITS

These are crumbly, savory morsels. Enjoy them with poached eggs, or buttered along side soups.

1 cup sunflower meal *(p. 150)*   1/2 cup butter or substitute**
1/4 cup flax meal   1 Tbs honey
1/2 cup coconut flour   1/2 tsp salt
2 Tbs mixed fresh herbs, minced fine*

1. Preheat oven to 350° F.

2. Place dry ingredients in a bowl. Mix them together using a pastry blender. Add butter, honey, and herbs and blend together until dry ingredients are just incorporated.

3. Place parchment paper on a sheet pan, and form 9 balls of dough. Space evenly on parchment-lined sheet pan.

4. Wet your hands and press balls of dough to 1/2" thick, to form biscuits. Bake for 20 to 25 minutes or until lightly brown and crisp. Cool 10 minutes or more before removing from pan. Serve warm.

Store any left over biscuits in an air tight container for up to 5 days.

**SCD option
Paleo option
GF
Nut-Free
DF option**

Options:

SCD option:
Use dairy-free butter. Substitute almond flour for sunflower meal, and omit flax meal and increase coconut flour by 1/4 cup.

Paleo option:
Use dairy-free butter.

* Use fresh, thyme, rosemary, sage, parsley, chives, and savory. Another nice variation is snipped dill.
If you don't have fresh herbs, use 2 tsp. dried.

Note:
**If using unsalted butter, increase salt to 3/4 tsp.

Options:

* If you don't have fresh rosemary, you may substitute 2 tsp dry rosemary.

Serve with:

• Navy bean hummus
• Roasted eggplant, tomatoes, peppers, zucchini, or other vegetables.
• Cheese or cheese substitutes
• Smoked fish

**If needed place in the freezer for 15 minutes to help remove top sheet.

Notes:

Flax meal is very high in nickel. Avoid this recipe if you have a nickel allergy.

ROSEMARY-FLAX CRACKERS

There's nothing like a crunchy cracker for dips, savory spreads, or just snacking. These have sustained me through many a long hiking trip.

2 cup golden or dark flax meal
1 Tbls rosemary leaves, snipped*
1/2 tsp black sesame seeds
1/4 tsp poppy seeds

1/2 tsp sea salt
1/2 tsp garlic powder
1 cup water

1. Prehead oven to 400° F.

2. Mix together dry ingredients with a pastry blender/cutter or wooden spoon. Add water, 1/4 cup at a time mixing well between additions. Let sit for 5 minutes.

3. Place a piece of parchment paper the size of your largest sheet pan on the counter. Press the cracker dough into a rectangle in the center of the parchment. Place a piece of waxed paper on top of the dough. Using a rolling pin or your hands, roll out the dough as thin as possible. Carefully remove the top sheet of paper.** Using a pizza cutter or long knife score the crackers in a grid according to the size and shape you prefer. Slide crackers with parchment onto baking sheet.

3. Bake on middle rack at 400° F for 25 minutes. Remove from oven and allow to cool long enough for you to flip the crackers over and break them apart. Remove any that are crisp to cool, then spread remaining crackers evenly over sheet pan. Lower the heat to 170° F, return to oven, and continue baking until dry and crisp, (this can take up to an hour or more).

4. Cool completely, then store for up to 2 weeks in an airtight container.

HONEY *Stories*

The first time Frederick came to visit, he met me after work at my house to pick up the kits for his bee hives. He had ordered the supplies through The Village Store where I worked. We moved the bits and pieces to his truck, then took a tour of the garden. He was intrigued by the various flowers and my tall stands of blooming mint. When he spotted my cat Griz, he was smitten (with the cat that is). They were to become life long pals. A few weeks later (we were dating by that time) Frederick suggested bringing the newly made hives to my yard. He thought the mint blooms would make a nice forage for bees.

The hives were prepared and the bees installed. And all seemed quite agreeable to the bees. The summer brought many adventures: evening walks on the beach with glowing footprints in the sand, courtesy of the bioluminescent comb jellies, bird walks to Wattuppa Reservoir at dawn to listen to a winter wren belting it out above a bubbling spring deep in the woods, and bee wrangling.

Late one afternoon, I got a call from a fellow employee at The Village Store. There was a swarm of honey bees in the Linden tree above the parking lot. Frederick called local bee keeper Clark Chase, who told us to meet him there in 15 minutes. We only had one bee suit, but quickly grabbed it and a smoker. We need not have bothered. Clark explained that when the bees swarm, they are very docile. We parked the truck directly under the swarm, and all three of us stood on the truck bed. Clark had us hold the hive box just below the swarm, and using the sturdy handle of a spade, gave the tree branch a sharp whack. The entire swarm dropped into the hive box, and he quickly slid the top on.

By November, the bees at my house had settled in for a long winter's nap. Little did they know there were moving plans in their future. Frederick and I were engaged at that point, and I was selling my house. The bees would be moving to River Rock Farm along with me. After our swarm experience, we didn't think this would be a difficult task. At nightfall we applied some smoke to calm the bees and carefully loaded both hives into the truck. The bees were starting to pay attention, and the volume of buzzing increased as we started the engine. I followed behind in my red Jetta. The bees were not pleased. We had put a cover on their hive entrances, but still bees were trickling out. By the time we got to their new location, the hives were positively vibrating. Frederick left them in the truck bed to settle down before moving them into place. We quickly escaped into the house to let them simmer down. A few hours later, the hives had resumed a low hum, but there were honey bees covering my red Jetta. We moved the hives *121* into place and opened the entrances, and by morning, they were happily sunning themselves.

Honey takes on the flavors of the plants the bees are pollinating. The following spring the hives were moved yet again to the edge of the cow pasture. The bees happily settled in to their new spot. Their primary forage was clethra, or sweet pepper bush. That first batch of honey was delightfully minty and light in color. Later in the summer the hives became surrounded by goldenrod, and asters. We harvested a small batch before the autumn became too cold. This honey was nearly inedible. It was dark, and smelled of dirty socks with fishy over tones. It turns out golden rod is not a desirable forage for honey. This got us doing some research. We learned that holly blossoms lend an orange marmalade flavor to honey, while rhododenron honey can actually be mildly toxic.

When our son Ben went on a field trip for his Land Journeys and Ethics class in New Zealand, he learned many things about navigation, survival, native species, and geology. But he also discovered some interesting qualities about a very special type of honey. Most honey is produced when a honey bee gathers pollen and nectar from a flowering plant. Honey produced using the flowers of the manuka tree are probably the most valuable honey, as it has been shown to have antibacterial, antiviral and anti-inflammatory properties. But while the group of students walked through a black beech forest, Ben's professor pointed out the strange white filaments protruding from the trunks of the beech trees. He encouraged everyone to take a taste from the glistening droplets at the end of each filament. Ben found it to be sweet. Beech honeydew is a non-pollen honey produced with the help of insects attacking black and red beech trees on the South Island of New Zealand. The white filament is actually the tail end of the insect. The pressurized sap of the beech tree is secreted by the insect and the droplets of beech sap nectar are gathered by honeybees to produce a uniquely flavored dark honey.

Sourcing honey takes a bit of care. Because honey contains naturally occurring enzymes, it's easily digestible and is less likely to cause gut problems. It's best not to heat honey above 170°F. Raw honey has not been heated, and the enzymes remain. I do use honey in my baked goods, but because it is actually sweeter than cane sugar, I need to use a smaller amount.

I have found over the years that I must be careful about sourcing the honey. There have been studies showing that some honey purveyors have been adding corn syrup to increase their profits. There are two good tests to determine if you have pure honey. If it crystallizes it's probably pure. If it dissolves easily in cold water, it is not pure. I was quite dismayed when I found a honey I had been using was likely adulterated.

Another factor to consider when choosing your honey is pesticides. Bees will forage up to five miles from their hives. It is thought that colony collapse, or the death of an entire hive of bees could be caused by certain pesticides called neonicotinoids. I now order raw honey from places that have rigorous organic farming standards. I can taste the difference!

Drinks & Teas

TEAS

Roasted Dandelion Root *125*
Lemon Balm *125*
Rose Petal & Lavender *127*
Fresh Mint *127*
Lavender Lemon Balm-ade *127*

SMOOTHIES

Blueberry Nutmeg *129*
Mango Carrot *129*
Chocolate Banana Cinnamon *130*

Options:

There are many brands of dandelion tea; but if you'd like something really rich, look for Teechino's Dandelion Dark Roast.

A Note on Making Tea

Steeping tea in a pot really does add to its flavor and health benefits. The process of steeping holds in the essential oils and keeps the water hotter for longer to extract the most from the leaves or roots.

Roasted Dandelion Root Tea

Dandelion is a bitter herb and is supposed to aid digestion. It's a wonderful substitute for coffee. While you can certainly dig and roast your own roots, roasted dandelion root tea is now readily available. Makes 1 serving.

1 tea bag of roasted dandelion root tea*
10 oz. of boiling water.
2 Tbs of half-and-half or substitute
1 tsp honey or to taste

1. Place tea bag in a a small pot or a mug covered with a lid. Pour boiling water over tea bag. Steep tea for 5 or more minutes.

2. If using a tea pot, pour into a large mug, or remove tea bag. Add half-and-half and honey and stir well.

Lemon Balm Tea

If you're lucky enough to have fresh lemon balm growing in your yard, the leaves make a delightful tea. Lemon balm is said to have a calming affect. Dried lemon balm has a very different flavor, but is equally as good.

1. Lightly stuff a tea pot with washed lemon balm leaves and stems. Add boiling water and cover. Allow to steep for 5 or more minutes. Serve with honey.

126

If it worked for Peter Rabbit, it may work for you.

If you've had a bad day, or need to relax, pluck a handful of chamomile blossoms and cover with boiling water. The smell alone will leave you smiling.

ROSE PETAL & LAVENDER TEA

Making your own tea mixes is fun. Just do some research. Herbs can have desirable or undesirable affects depending on your condition. Makes 2 to 3 servings.

1 Tbs each of fresh rose petals and lavender leaves or flowers
20 oz. of water
Honey to taste

1. Steep tea in pot for 5 or more minutes.

2. Pour into tea cups or mugs through a stainer. Add honey and stir well.

FRESH MINT TEA

Mint tea is said to aid digestion. There are many varieties of mint. Some of my favorites for tea are spearmint, chocolate mint, orange mint, and banana mint. Dried mint is equally good for tea, just use 1/2 Tbs per serving.

1. Lightly stuff a tea pot with washed fresh mint leaves and stems. Add boiling water and cover. Allow to steep for 5 or more minutes. Serve with honey.

LAVENDER LEMON BALM-ADE

This makes a pretty pink and refreshing cold drink. Makes 6 servings.

2 Tbs lavender blossoms dried
2 Tbs hibiscus flowers dried
1/4 cup fresh lemon balm, or 2 Tbs dried
6 cups of boiling water
1/2 cup honey or to taste
fresh lemon balm and Johnny Jumpups for garnish (optional)
Ice

1. Mix together lavender, hibiscus and lemon balm in a large pan. Add boiling water, cover and simmer for 10 minutes. Turn off heat, keep covered, and allow to cool. Strain into a large pitcher and add honey to taste, stir well. Refrigerate until cold. Serve with ice and garnishes.

128

Option:

* Cultured Dairy
Yogurt is fine on the
SCD.

Smoothies

If you have a stick blender smoothies are quick and easy. You can also use a juicer, blender, or food processor. Experiment with other fresh or frozen fruits.

BLUEBERRY NUTMEG SMOOTHIE

This can be made with fresh blueberries, but the frozen berries help to thicken the smoothie. Makes 1 generous serving.

8 oz plain yogurt or substitute*
3/4 cup of frozen blueberries
1 to 2 Tbs honey or to taste
1/2 tsp nutmeg

1. Place all ingredients in a deep measuring cup or carafe for a stick blender or into blender or food processor bowl. Blend for 30 to 45 seconds, or until smooth.

2. Add a dusting of additional nutmeg on top for garnish.

MANGO CARROT SMOOTHIE

This bright sunny smoothie is a wonderful summer pick-me-up.
Makes 1 generous serving.

8 oz plain yogurt or substitute*
1/2 cup frozen mango**
2 large pitted dates or 2 Tbs honey or to taste
1/4 cup shredded fresh carrot

1. Place all ingredients in a deep measuring cup or carafe for a stick blender or into blender or food processor bowl. Blend for 30 to 45 seconds, or until smooth.

Options:

* Cultured Dairy
Yogurt is fine on the
SCD.

**Combine fresh
or frozen pineapple
or banana with the
mango.

Chocolate Banana Cinnamon Smoothie

A satisfying snack or dessert. Makes 1 generous serving.

8 oz plain yogurt or substitute *
1 ripe frozen banana
2 large pitted dates or 2 Tbs honey or to taste
1/4 avocado *(optional)*
2 Tbs unsweetened cocoa powder or carob powder *
1 tsp cinnamon

1. Place all ingredients in a deep measuring cup, carafe, or blender. Blend for 30 to 45 seconds, or until smooth.

SCD option
Paleo
GF
Nut Free
DF option

Options:

*SCD option: Dairy Yogurt is fine on the SCD, but omit cocoa or carob powder

Notes:
Chocolate and avocados are very high in nickel. Eat them sparingly if you have a nickel allergy.

FINDING FOOD in New Zealand

In July of 2017 my son, Ben, took a semester abroad at the University of Canterbury in Christchurch, New Zealand. The two of us had spent 5 years homeschooling, and it only felt natural for me to go along. The plan was for a 5 month stay, with Frederick joining us for 3 weeks in November.

After our 38 hour journey with a stopover in Sydney to visit the zoo, we arrived in New Zealand late at night. We were rather incoherent and went right to bed. The next morning when we woke our hosts, the Beckners, had some basics on hand for us. After enjoying our breakfast of scrambled eggs and fried onions, it was off to the shops. Despite our jet lag, on day one, it was imperative that we began our quest for foods that we could eat.

Danielle Beckner had grown up in our hometown of Dartmouth, MA, and had been living in New Zealand with her husband Clay and two children for 4 years. Danielle and the kids found us quite amusing as we wove our way, barely conscious, through the aisles. They finally resorted to linking arms with us to cross the street, as we were not good at seeing where the cars were coming from, and had very slow reflexes. I eventually got over my jet lag, and by day four even managed to learn to drive our rental car on the correct side of the road (most of the time), with Ben chanting, "Stay Left" at every intersection.

I didn't really know what to expect when it came to New Zealand cuisine. Lamb was certainly a commonly used meat, and barbecue (or "barbie" as the Kiwi's call it) was a popular cooking method. But on that first day, when I ventured into our neighborhood New World grocery store, I couldn't get over the size of the produce. I felt like I had become a Hobbit, as I hefted a nearly yard long head of celery and 2 pound carrot. Then there were the kiwi fruits. They had the green kiwi I was accustomed to, but the golden kiwis were more sweet than tart, and had overtones of pineapple. I was soon to learn the fruits and vegetables also tasted better. Most were New Zealand grown, picked ripe and not shipped from half way around the world. I also discovered, they only stocked enough of the more perishable produce to last the day. By 6:00 pm the lettuce, bananas and berries were usually gone, leaving empty shelves until the next morning.

The grocery store seafood offerings were varied and fresh, as you might expect on an island. The meat department commonly offered venison and many cuts of lamb. However most of the sausages contained sugars and starches, and the dairy section had limited choices for cheese varieties. Then we discovered the specialty foods department. We found wonderful cheeses from the White Stone Cheese Company in Oamaru. The double cream and butter from Lewis Road Creamery was rich and flavorful. The alternative flours and granolas were imaginative, and the raw kiwi vinegar was bright and tart. I was surprised to find the eggs were offered up on shelves next to the cereals, no refrigeration necessary. But a grocery store doesn't represent the local foods.

The Beckners brought us to many of their favorite food haunts. We immediately fell in love with a health food store named Pico, with it's bins of dried bananas, and unsweetened coconut from Sri Lanka. The staff pre-bagged a variety of spices, dried fruits, and raw cocoa butter. They milled various seeds and grains and offered them in a refrigerated case. Honeys and oils were dispensed into recycled jars, or you could bring your own container. I quickly learned to take a sniff before dispensing the honey into a recycled pickle jar to be sure it didn't retain any hints of garlic. They offered some grain-free pastas made from black beans, wonderful beet and sweet potato chips, plus almond crackers and cookies that Ben couldn't get enough of. There was a tempting display on the counter featuring their staff's daily whims in vegan baked goods, and homemade chocolates.

We visited the Opawa Farmers Market that first weekend, and got introduced to the local farmers and vendors. I learned kumara was the Maori name the native New Zealand people use for sweet potato. Originating in South America, the kumara was probably carried here by Polynesians via Hawaii. One Maori farmer carried nothing but heirloom varieties of kumara, some as large as a guinea pig. These gigantic tubers were much more varied than the sweet potatoes and yams I was accustomed to. There were some that were purple on the outside and marbled with creamy white and pink on the inside; others were bright red and yellow. Since it was late winter, we marveled at the flower stalls with freshly cut protea, and organic farms selling everything from pumpkins and salad greens to herb plants. While we enjoyed the violin solo played by a local student, we tasted some of the cheeses offered by the Emilio family. Two generations of Emilios made the most delicious cheeses we tasted while we were in New Zealand. Most were based on traditional Italian recipes, but occasionally they would throw in their take on Swiss, or add some caraway seeds to a soft cheese.

Next it was off to the butchers. Banfields of Beckenam became our go-to for meats. They were friendly and specialized in sustainably grown, grass-fed meats of high quality at a reasonable price. Their pork fillets (tenderloins) were amazingly tender and delicious. A visit to Banfields was always memorable. Peter the butcher would tell us about the farms where the meats came from, ask how I was planning to prepare the meats, and we exchanged recipes

and sympathized about each other's allergies. He greeted most customers by name and brought our purchases around the counter, and opened the door before handing us the bag and wishing us a heartfelt "Good day".

New Zealand cuisine, it turned out, was a melting pot of cultures, with a strong focus on delicious fresh ingredients. While a Kiwi would also enjoy hearty helpings of meat pies and sweet baked goods, we were quite content and impressed with the simple foods we prepared from the vastly superior food products gleaned from the volcanic soils and coastal waters of New Zealand. *132*

Basics & Extras

133

134

Basil Pesto

When basil is in season, I have a jar of homemade pesto in the fridge at all times. It adds flavor to sauces, dressings, salads, and even egg dishes.

1/4 cup sunflower seeds
1 large garlic clove sliced
1/2 tsp salt

2 cups loosely packed basil leaves
1/2 cup olive oil or more

**SCD option
Paleo
GF
Nut-Free
DF option**

Options:
• For a lighter pesto, replace basil with mint, and garlic with 1 Tbs onion.

• You can also use parsley and lemon balm in place of the basil for fish dishes.

SCD option:
Substitute pine nuts for the sunflower seeds.

1. Have a clean, air-tight container ready. Basil oxidizes when crushed, so the sooner you get it sealed up the greener it will stay.

2. Place sunflower seeds, garlic, and salt in the bowl of a food processor or blender. Pulse to roughly chop ingredients.

3. Add basil leaves, and process until finely chopped. Scrape down sides. Add olive oil in a stream, while processing. Add additional olive oil if needed to make a loose paste. When well mixed, place in air-tight container. Drizzle additional olive oil over the top to cover the pesto. This will keep the pesto green. Cover and refrigerate until ready to use.

Homemade Garlic Mayonnaise

Options:

Tartar Sauce
1/2 cup mayonnaise
1 small red onion
1/2 stalk celery
1 Tbs red pepper
1 Tbs parsley
2 tsp honey
1 tsp sherry vinegar

Chop fine onion, celery, pepper and parsley. Mix all ingredients together, and refrigerate until ready to use.

Dill Sauce
1/2 cup mayonnaise
1 small red onion
1/4 cup fresh dill
(or 2 Tbs dried)
1 tsp sherry vinegar

Combine minced onion, dill and vinegar. Let sit for 10 minutes. Stir into mayonnaise.

Note:
Consuming raw eggs may increase your risk of food borne illness, especially if you have certain medical conditions.

This simple mayonnaise is the basis for so many good dishes. Use as a topping for burgers, eggs, or fish. Lightly blanch fresh string beans, asparagus, and carrot spears to dip into this aioli sauce. Mix into tuna, or diced chicken to top a hearty salad. And, it's delightful on a portobello mushroom "burger"!

1 small garlic clove minced
2 egg yolks
2 tsp sherry *(or other)* vinegar
1 Tbs Dijon mustard
1 Tbs water

1/4 tsp pepper
1/4 tsp salt
1/2 cup sunflower oil
1/4 cup olive oil

1. Place garlic, egg yolks, vinegar, mustard, salt, and pepper in the bowl of a food processor or blender. (Don't add the oil until reading step 2.) Pulse to combine. Using a spatula to scrape the bottom and sides of bowl.

2. Replace top, and remove center hole cover. While the motor is running, add the oils in a thin stream very slowly. Pause to scrape down the sides of the bowl occasionally. Continue slowly adding the oil and process until thick, using additional oil if needed to make a smooth thick sauce. Refrigerate until ready to use.

Pesto Mayonnaise

Stir together equal portions of pesto and mayonnaise. Refrigerate.

KETCHUP

GF
Nut-Free
DF

Note:
There are some commercially available ketchups that don't contain sugar.

This sauce is thick, sweet tangy and spicy.

1 Tbs olive oil	1/3 cup cider vinegar
1 medium onion chopped	1/2 tsp smoked sea salt
1 clove garlic, chopped	1/2 tsp ground cloves
1 26 oz jar of tomato puree	1/2 tsp ground allspice
1/3 cup honey	1/4 cup raisins

1. Place the olive oil in a saucepan over medium high heat. Add the onion and garlic. Saute until transparent and lightly browned.

2. Add the remaining ingredients and bring to a simmer.

3. Lower heat to mediumlow and continue simmering, stirring occasionally until thickened, approximately 30 minutes.

4. Allow to cool slightly. Using a food processor, or food mill, puree until very smooth.

5. Use immediately or store in an air-tight glass jar in the refrigerator for up to 1 month.

SCD option
Paleo option
GF
Nut-Free
Low Nickel
DF option

Options:

*SCD & Paleo:
Use ghee or dairy-free butter.

*Low Nickel:
Use dairy butter

Dill Butter
Replace herbs with 1/4 cup fresh dill snipped, or 3 Tbs dried dill.

Sage Butter:
Add 4 fresh sage leaves chopped to the herb mix for use in basting turkey.

HERBED BUTTER

The butter and oil absorb the essential oils of the fresh herbs. I love cooking with herbed butter as it infuses an entire dish with flavor. It also makes a wonderful topping for vegetables.

1 cup butter or substitute*
6 chives snipped
1 sprig rosemary snipped
1/2 tsp salt *(optional)*

2 Tbs olive oil
3 sprigs thyme leaves
2 sprigs parsley chopped

1. Allow butter to soften at room temperature. Place in a mixing bowl or food processor. Add olive oil, herbs, and salt if using unsalted butter. Mix well and place in covered container.

2. Spread on herb biscuits, over sauteed or steamed vegetables, on eggs, to season soups and sauces, and more.

3. Store any leftovers in a covered container in the refrigerator.

CREPES

Options:

*SCD & Paleo:
Use dairy-free half-and-half and butter.

*Low Nickel:
Use dairy half-and-half and butter

* You may substitute another non-dairy creamer for the half-and-half, but a thicker consistency milk or cream makes a sturdier crepe.

We enjoy these for breakfast folded up with plain yogurt and fruit preserves. They can also be filled with fresh fruit and pastry cream for dessert, or used to wrap savory fillings like Chicken Curry with Fruit (page 83) for brunch.

6 eggs
1 cup half-and-half or substitute*
1/4 tsp salt

1 Tbs or more of butter for pan
3 Tbs coconut flour
1/4 tsp cinnamon *(optional)*

1. Place eggs, half-and-half, salt and coconut flour in food processor, and blend until smooth. Let sit for 15 minutes. (You may also use a whisk and bowl, but beat well.)

2. Heat 1 tsp of butter in non-stick skillet over medium high heat. Pour 2 Tbs of batter into the center, then pick up skillet and quickly swirl to coat the bottom of the pan. Fill in any gaps with a small amount of additional batter.

3. Cook for 1 to 2 minutes or until the edges look dry and browned. Using a spatula lift the edge of the crepe and fold in half. Lift the other corner and fold in half again, then remove to a serving plate. Repeat with the remaining batter, adding more butter as needed. (If crepes stick to pan, raise the heat.)

4. Serve folded with toppings or unfold and place fillings along the center, and roll up before serving.

Sponge Cake

A delicious cake served with fresh fruit or for bread pudding.

1 cup water
1/2 cup butter or substitute*
2 Tbs honey

3/4 cup coconut flour
4 large eggs separated
1/4 tsp salt

1. Preheat oven to 400° F. Line a rimmed baking sheet with parchment.

2. In a saucepan bring water and butter to a boil for 3 minutes. Lower heat to medium, add coconut flour, and stir until mixture is smooth. Remove from heat and let cool briefly.

3. Place egg whites in mixer with whisk attachment. Whip until soft peaks form. Remove to a large bowl and put aside.

4. Place egg yolks, honey, salt and coconut flour mixture in mixer and whisk together to make a thick batter. Stop mixer and remove bowl. Add whipped egg whites to top of batter in mixer bowl. Using a spatula, gently fold egg whites into batter. Spread evenly on parchment lined baking sheet to 1/2" thickness.

5. Bake at 400° F for 15 to 20 minute, or until light golden brown and puffed. Turn off heat, crack door open and allow to cool in oven, before removing from parchment.

SCD option
Paleo option
GF
Nut-Free
Spice-Free
DF option

Option:
*SCD & Paleo:
Use dairy-free butter. Use dairy-free toppings.

Note:
This light airy cake is great on it's own, however it also has many uses:

• Brush it with sherry, layer it with berries, fruit preserves, pastry cream and whipped cream to make a Trifle.

• Layer with ice cream, freeze, slice and serve with fruit or chocolate sauce

• Use in Tiramisu or Bread Pudding.

140

SIMPLE PASTRY CREAM

SCD option
Paleo option
GF
Nut-Free
Low Nickel**
DF

This pastry cream can be made with any full-fat milk or milk substitute, such as coconut creamer, or almond milk. Pastry cream can be used to fill crepes, between layers of sponge cake in a trifle, or as a topping for cakes.

5 egg yolks   1/2 cup honey
2 cups heavy cream or substitute*   1/4 tsp salt
1/2 tsp flavoring *(nutmeg, cinnamon, vanilla, or rum)*

1. Place cream and salt in a medium-sized sauce pan. Bring to a low simmer over medium heat.

2. In a small bowl whisk together egg yolks. Add 1 cup of cream, slowly to the egg yolks, whisking continuously. Then, while whisking the cream in the saucepan, slowly pour the egg yolk and cream mixture back into the sauce pan.

3. Return saucepan to heat over medium low, and cook for about 10 minutes or until thickened enough to coat the back of a spoon. Whisk continuously, and lower heat if it starts bubbling.

4. Remove from heat and stir in flavoring of choice. Pour into a bowl and let cool. Cover and refrigerate.

Options:

*SCD & Paleo:
Substitute other non-dairy milks for the heavy cream.
**Remember coconut milk is very high in nickel. Use dairy cream if avoiding nickel.

Notes:

What do you do with all those egg whites? Use them to batter fried fish on page 81. Or try making the dacquoise on page 114. Refrigerate the egg whites until ready to use.

Making Your Own

If you are not able to find some of the ingredients listed in the recipes, I've included instructions for making your own here, and in the side bar on some recipes.

Date Syrup

A great substitute for molasses; it is equally as nutritious and sweet.

2 cup pitted dates chopped
2 cup water

1. Place dates and water into a sauce pan over medium high heat. Cover and bring to a simmer, then lower heat to medium low. Cook stirring occasionally until dates are mushy and the liquid is thickened.

2. Remove from heat and pour through cheese cloth or strainer into a container with a lid. Reserve date solids to make Date Paste and/or Date Sugar.

3. Refrigerate any leftovers. If crystallized, reheat over low heat before using.

Date Paste

Place the date solids left over from making date syrup into a food processor and puree until smooth. Store in an airtight container in the refrigerator.

Date Sugar

Because I live in a humid climate, I have not had good luck making my own date sugar. However if you have a coffee grinder and you'd like to try, you'll need to start by making date paste.

1. Preheat oven to lowest setting or 170° F.

2. Place a sheet of parchment paper on a baking sheet. Spread 1 cup of date paste evenly across the parchment to a thickness of 1/8" or less.

3. Bake until the date paste is very dry and cracks when bent. Cool completely. ❋

4. Break into small pieces and process in a coffee grinder or food processor into a fine powder. Store in a tightly sealed container for up to 2 weeks.

Paleo
GF
Nut-Free
DF

Note:
Pre-made date syrup, paste, and sugar are available from some health food stores.

❋When making date sugar, it is important to keep it very dry throughout the process. If the date sugar sticks together, dry in an oven at 170° F for 15 minutes. Allow it to cool and grind again.

Dates are moderately high in nickel. Use them sparingly if you have a nickel allergy.

142

CRANBERRY SAUCE

SCD
Paleo
GF
Low Nickel
Nut-Free
Spice-Free
DF

Options:

* If you're not a fan of tart cranberry sauce, add more honey.

This is so easy to make. I look forward to autumn when local organic cranberries are available. I am lucky to live in an area where I can forage for wild cranberries! This sauce is delicious on turkey burgers, roasted chicken, turkey and duck.

2 cups fresh cranberries, stems removed and rinsed
(or frozen organic cranberries)
1 large or 2 medium cooking apples, peeled and diced
1/4 to 1/2 cup honey*
1 Tbs water
1/4 tsp salt

1. Place all ingredients in a non-reactive sauce pan.

2. Cover and bring to a simmer over medium-high heat for 15 minutes, or until cranberries begin to pop and apples are soft.

3. Remove cover, raise heat to high, and bring to a rolling boil for 2 minutes. Stir until sauce is smooth and thickened.

4. Serve warm, or for a thicker sauce allow it cool.

5. Refrigerate any leftovers in a glass container.

SCD
Paleo
GF
Nut-Free
DF option

Options:
This is wonderful when using pine-apple in place of the mango.

Note:
*You may also use dried mango in place of fresh.
Place 10 slices of dried mango in flat bottomed, heat-proof bowl, and pour enough boiling water over to cover. Let sit for 1 hour, drain and cut into small pieces, and proceed with recipe.

Mango Salsa

This is delicious on grilled chicken, or fish.

1 1/2 cups fresh mango, peeled and diced small
(or defrost frozen mango and cut small) *
2 scallions, green and white parts sliced thin
2 Tbs chopped fresh cilantro
1 Tbs honey
1 Tbs sunflower oil
1/4 tsp salt

1. Place all ingredients in a small bowl, and stir together. Let sit for 20 minutes for flavors to blend.

2. Serve at room temperature, and refrigerate any leftovers in a glass container for up to 1 week.

BALSAMIC VINAIGRETTE

SCD
Paleo
GF
Low Nickel
Nut-Free
DF

Options:

* You can use red wine or sherry vinegar in place of the balsamic vinegar.

Creamy Vinaigrette Dressing:

In a small bowl whisk to combine equal parts balsamic vinaigrette and home-made garlic mayonnaise. Store any leftovers in the refrigerator.

This dressing is an excellent staple to have on hand. It's equally good on salads or used as a marinade.

2 tsp Dijon mustard
1/4 cup balsamic vinegar*
3/4 cup olive oil or sunflower oil
1/4 tsp salt and freshly ground pepper

1. Place mustard, vinegar, salt, and pepper in a glass bottle with a top that seals well. Shake well.

2. Add olive oil to bottle and seal. Shake vigorously until all ingredients are incorporated.

3. Serve immediately or refrigerate for up to 1 month.

SCD
Paleo
GF
Nut-Free
DF
Vegetarian

Options:

*If you can tolerate citrus fruit you can substitute lime juice for the sherry vinegar.

Note:

Traditional hummus is made with garbanzo beans; however, these are high in starches that can cause inflammation. Navy beans are a healthy substitute.

Beans are very high in nickel. Eat them sparingly if you have a nickel allergy.

Navy Bean Hummus

This is delicious with Rosemary-Flax Crackers, or fresh vegetables.

1 - 15oz can of navy beans, rinsed and drained
1 scallion sliced thin, white part only (reserve green part for garnish)
1/3 cup olive oil   1 medium garlic clove, minced
1 Tbs chopped fresh cilantro   1 Tbs sherry vinegar*
1/2 tsp ground cumin   1/4 tsp salt and pepper to taste
1/8 tsp cayenne pepper *(optional)*

1. Heat a small sauce pan on medium-low heat. Add olive oil, white part of scallion and garlic. Swirl just long enough for the garlic to begin to cook and release some fragrance. Be careful not to brown the garlic or it will be bitter. Remove from heat, and cool slightly.

2. Place all ingredients including the cooled olive oil mixture in a food processor bowl. Pulse to blend together. Add the olive oil mixture slowly in a steady stream while blending. Scrape down sides and continue blending until smooth. Taste and correct seasonings.

3. Garnish with thin-sliced green scallions. Serve chilled or at room temperature.

4. Refrigerate any leftovers in a glass container for up to 1 week.

HONEY MUSTARD MARINADE

SCD
Paleo
GF
Low Nickel
Nut-Free
DF

Options:

* If using venison steaks, marinate over night in the refrigerator.

I use this marinade on boneless chicken breasts, pork tenderloins and even venison steaks. The sliced garlic sticks to the meat and adds a sweet, garlicky note every few bites.

1 Tbs Dijon mustard
1 Tbs sunflower oil or olive oil
1 Tbs honey
2 garlic cloves sliced thin
1/2 tsp dried thyme

2 boneless chicken breasts, or pork tenderloins

1. Place mustard, sunflower oil, honey and garlic in a bowl large enough to hold the meat you are marinading. Stir the marinade until smooth.

2. Add your meat of choice to the marinade bowl and toss well to coat.

3. Cover bowl and place in the refrigerator for 2 hours or up to 6 hours. *

4. We like to cook over a fire pit using maple logs. Start the fire at least 1 hour ahead so that you have a nice bed of very hot coals, but no big flames. If you are using a propane grill, preheat to medium.

5. When your fire is ready, place meat in a fish grill, or grilling basket. Coat the top of the meat with any remaining marinade or garlic slices. Close the basket.

6. Place over hot coals for approximately 10 minutes per side, or until nicely browned and cooked through. Cool for 5 minutes before serving.

Pizza Crust

This makes a thin crunchy pizza crust.

1 cup sunflower meal	1 tsp dried oregano
1/2 cup coconut flour	1 tsp dried thyme
1/4 cup golden flax meal	2 Tbs olive oil
1 tsp salt	2 large eggs, beaten

1. Preheat oven to 400° F. Line a large rimmed sheet pan with parchment paper.

2. Place all dry ingredients in a medium sized bowl. Using a pastry blender, blend dry ingredients together.

3. In a small bowl mix together eggs and olive oil. Slowly add the egg mixture to the dry ingredients while blending with the pastry blender. Continue mixing until dry ingredients are incorporated, if needed, adding water until it forms a dough.

4. Place dough on prepared parchment paper. Using your hands, press into a circle or rectangle until dough is 1/8" to 1/4" thick. (You may also place another piece of parchment on top and use a rolling pin.)

5. Bake crust for 12 to 15 minutes or until lightly browned and firm. Remove from oven and add toppings of choice and bake at 400° F for 10 minutes more.

SCD option
GF
Nut-Free
DF

Options:

SCD option:
Replace the sunflower and flax meal with almond flour.

Toppings:
- Roasted tomatoes
- Olives
- Prosciutto
- Sliced mushrooms
- Onions
- Peppers
- Cooked sausage
- Roasted eggplant
- Roasted peppers
- Grilled artichokes
- Pesto

Notes:
Sunflower seeds are very high in nickel. Eat them sparingly if you have a nickel allergy.

TOASTED SUNFLOWER SEEDS

Paleo
GF
Nut-Free
DF

Options:

❉ You may substitute olive oil for the sunflower oil.

Notes:

Sunflower seeds are very high in nickel. Use sparingly if you have a nickel allergy.

These are a bit like popped corn: once you start nibbling, it's hard to stop. They make a wonderful crunchy addition to salads.

1 1/2 cup shelled sunflower seeds
1 Tbs sunflower oil❉
1/2 tsp salt

1. Heat a 12" skillet on medium heat. Add oil and salt and swirl together.

2. Pour in sunflower seeds, and toss to coat with oil and salt.

3. Using a spatula or wooden spoon spread the seeds evenly over the bottom of the pan.

4. Continue toasting and stirring, and flattening every few minutes.

5. When fragrant and lightly brown remove from heat.

6. Allow to cool completely before storing in an airtight container.

**Paleo
GF
Nut-Free
DF**

Options:

Pre-made sunflower flour or meal is available in some areas. It tends to be finer, and sometimes drier if the oil has been pressed out before grinding.

Notes:

Sunflower seeds are very high in nickel. Use sparingly if you have a nickel allergy.

Sunflower Meal

This is a highly nutritious alternative to flour. Sunflower seeds are especially high in the antioxidants, vitamin E, and selenium.

Sunflower Seeds are not recommended on the Specific Carbohydrate Diet (SCD), and can be substituted with almond flour in any recipe.

Sunflower meal turns a bright green color in baked goods, so don't be alarmed if you end up with shamrock colored food. It is only the chlorophyll in the sunflower reacting with the baking soda, and is perfectly harmless.

2 cups shelled sunflower seeds

1. Place sunflower seeds in a food processor or blender. Process at high speed for a minute or two, until very fine.

(I use ear protectors while making my sunflower meal. It can be pretty noisy.)

2. Use immediately, or store in an airtight container in the refrigerator for up to 1 month.

Green Pea Pasta

Notes:

❋ You may need to add more green pea flour if the dough is too sticky, so have some in reserve.

Ravioli Fillings:

• Dairy: Ricotta mixed with herbs, grated parmesan, and egg. Serve with roasted tomato sauce.

• Pureed butternut squash mixed with salt, pepper, and ground sage. Serve with whole sage leaves crisped in browned butter.

• Prosciutto and spinach minced and mixed with finely chopped sauted onion.

Avoid using raw meats in ravioli filling. Use only good quality fresh eggs.

This pasta is fun and easy to make. You can turn it into ravioli, lasagna or fettuccine. Just be aware, it tastes bitter prior to cooking. It's perfectly delicious once cooked.

100 grams *(approx. 3/4 cup)* sprouted green pea flour❋
1 medium-sized egg
1 Tbs olive oil or water as needed

1. Place pea flour and egg in a bowl and mix with your hands. Add just enough olive oil and/or water to form a stiff dough. Knead briefly and wrap in a slightly damp clean towel or plastic wrap. Let rest for 1/2 hour or store in the refrigerator until ready to use.

2. Bring dough to room temperature. If dry, wrap with moistened towel for 15 minutes. Dust a piece of parchment with pea or coconut flour. Place pasta dough on parchment and dust with more flour. Place a second piece of parchment on top, and roll out to a very thin sheet. (The thinner the better).

3. Cut into desired shape. Cook in rapidly boiling salted water for 3 minutes, or until it floats and is just tender. Drain and rinse with cold water before serving.

FOR RAVIOLI: Place 1 tsp of filling of choice 2" apart, on a 4" wide sheet of pasta. Brush pasta dough with lightly beaten egg along seams, fold over and seal edges. Press firmly with fingers or a fork. Lower 4 ravioli at a time, gently into boiling salted water, and cook until they float. Remove with a slotted spoon, and place in colander. Drizzle with a bit of olive oil to prevent sticking. Repeat with remaining ravioli. Serve warm with savory white sauce or tomato sauce.

Savory White Sauce

This take on traditional béchamel sauce tastes most authentic with dairy cream, but I enjoy it prepared with coconut creamer.

1 clove garlic minced
1 1/2 Tbs olive oil
1 Tbs coconut flour
1 1/2 cups heavy cream*
1 egg beaten

1/4 tsp each salt and pepper
1 tsp mixed dry Italian herbs
(or 1 Tbs of fresh herbs such as thyme, oregano, and parsley)
1 cup grated parmesan cheese**

1. In a small bowl whisk together cream and egg. Put aside.

2. Heat a small sauce pan over medium heat. Saute garlic in olive oil for 1 minute. Add coconut flour and stir until well mixed. Cook for 1 minute.

3. Reduce heat to low. Slowly add cream mixture to sauce pan while whisking. Keep at a low simmer for 2 to 3 minutes while stirring.

4. Add parmesan cheese (if using), herbs, salt, and pepper. Simmer on low heat until thickened, stirring continuously.

5. Use immediately as a sauce over eggs, pasta, or fish, as a filling in lasagna, or store in an airtight container in the refrigerator for up to 1 week.

Paleo option
GF
Nut-Free
Low Nickel
DF option

Options:

Paleo:
Substitute other non-dairy milks for the heavy cream.

Low Nickel
Coconut and nut milk are very high in nickel. Use dairy cream if avoiding nickel.

Diary Free:
Use coconut creamer or other non-dairy creamer, and omit the grated Parmesan cheese.

Note:

** It's best to grate your own cheese. Pre-grated cheeses often contains starches to prevent them from sticking.

152

APPENDIX & Resources

Food Cooperatives

Food cooperatives allow you to buy bulk foods and alternative ingredients that may not be available at your local grocery stores. They also connect like minded people, and allow them to work together to access healthy foods, while reducing shipping, packaging, and trips to the grocery store.

UNFI (United Natural Foods, Inc.)
Frontier Wholesale
Equal Exchange

To find food cooperatives search:
http://www.coopdirectory.org

Online Stores for Local Farms

Local Line offers an online shopping tool for local small farms. Ask your local farms or Town Agriculture Services for farms that participate.

Agricultural Extension System

For questions on gardening, agriculture, pesticides, and soil testing: https://ask2.extension.org

More info about Cooperative Extension Services:
https://nifa.usda.gov/cooperative-extension-system

Organic Farmers Associations

Search by state:
https://organicfarmersassociation.org

NOFA - Northeast Organic Farmers Association: https://nofa.org

Farmers Markets

Source healthy ingredients and develop meaningful relationships with local food producers.

153   Find your local farmers markets through:
https://www.ams.usda.gov/local-food-directories/farmersmarkets

Specific Carbohydrate Diet

The Specific Carbohydrate Diet (SCD) was developed by Elaine Gottschall, a biochemist and cell biologist, when her daughter was diagnosed with Crohn's disease. Her book *Breaking the Vicious Cycle* helped me and my son start our healing process. Later my husband benefited as well. While I didn't have significant gut disorders, I saw the value of reducing inflammation and strengthening the immune system and have stuck with the SCD for over 5 years.

About the Diet from *Breaking the Vicious Cycle Diet* website:
http://www.breakingtheviciouscycle.info/p/about-the-diet

Legal and Illegal Ingredient Listing from
Breaking the Vicious Cycle Diet website:
http://www.breakingtheviciouscycle.info/legal/listing

Other cookbooks for the SCD:
Eat Well, Feel Well by Kendall Conrad
Cooking for the Specific Carbohydrate Diet by Erica Kerwien

Paleo Diet

"The aim of a paleo diet is to return to a way of eating that's more like what early humans ate. The diet's reasoning is that the human body is genetically mismatched to the modern diet that emerged with farming practices — an idea known as the discordance hypothesis.

Farming changed what people ate and established dairy, grains, and legumes as additional staples in the human diet. This relatively late and rapid change in diet, according to the hypothesis, outpaced the body's ability to adapt. This mismatch is believed to be a contributing factor to the prevalence of obesity, diabetes, and heart disease today."
— *Excerpt from the Mayo Clinic website.*

What to eat
Fruits,vegetables, nuts, seeds, lean meats, especially grass-fed animals or wild game
Fish, especially those rich in omega-3 fatty acids: salmon, mackerel, albacore tuna
Oils from fruits and nuts, such as olive oil or walnut oil

What to avoid:
Grains, such as wheat, oats and barley, Legumes: beans, lentils, peanuts and peas
dairy products, refined sugar, salt, potatoes, and avoid highly processed foods in general

Other cookbooks for the Paleo Diet:
Against all Grain by Danielle Walker
Mediterranean Paleo Cooking by Caitlin Weeks, Nabil Boumrar & Diane Sanfillippo

Low Nickel Diet

There are many listings of nickel content in foods. There is also a great deal of contradictory information. I think this is due to the variability of nickel in foods that are tested. As I mentioned the nickel content will depend on the soil and environment the plant was grown in. Some plants and animal products are more likely to have a higher nickel content however. So it's best to do some research and get to know what to reduce or eliminate from your diet.

Some of the most useful information I have found is from rebelytics. They have an app that allows you to track your daily intake of nickel through a journal.

https://rebelytics.ca/nickelnavigator.html

You can also use the link to the pdf below to search for individual ingredients. This list includes the number of samples tested to gather the data, as well as, the minimum and maximum levels in the samples. This is helpful in better understanding the average nickel content in the listed foods.

https://rebelytics.ca/LND/lowNiDiet_r7.0_summaryTables.pdf

Jordan Taylor wrote a helpful book called *Nickel Allergy: The New Gluten*. It is full of facts about nickel allergies including testing, possible causes, sources of nickel exposure, and a listing of foods rated by their nickel content. Just be aware that this is not a complete listing and includes many whole meal items which can cause confusion.

While the focus of this cook book is what to eat, in the case of nickel allergy, there are definitely some ingredients that should be avoided.

Here are a few high-nickel ingredients to be aware of

Coconut
Because I was avoiding diary, grains, and nut flours, I was consuming a lot of coconut products. Initially I was told coconut was safe for those with allergies. Unfortunately it is extremely high in nickel. When I eliminated coconut products from my diet and skin products I saw an improvement. I have chosen to continue to use small amounts of coconut flour. It seems to be the lesser of the flour evils.

Sunflower Seeds
These protein rich seeds are packed with vitamin B6, Magnesium and Selenium. They can also have an extremely high nickel content. I had been using sunflower meal as an alternative to almond flour. I now try to limit this ingredient to infrequent treats.

Flax meal

Flaxseeds are high in omega 3. They also add healthy fiber to your diet. The flax meal produced by grinding flaxseeds is an excellent binding agent in grain-free cooking. Flaxseed also contains a moderately high nickel content, so I use it sparingly.

Legumes - Lentils, Beans, Soy and Peas

Legumes are a family of plants which produce seed pods with two halves, containing multiple round or oval high protein seeds. Lentils are a legume rich in fibre, folate and potassium. While lentil pasta is a convenient low carbohydrate alternative to wheat pasta, keep in mind that lentils are moderately high in nickel. This is also true for cooked and dried navy beans and peas.

Soy beans and soy products such as tofu, soy milk, soy flour, and soy additives are all very high in nickel. Even fresh and frozen green peas contain enough nickel to be a concern to those with a nickel allergy. Fresh cooked snow peas and green beans contain the lowest amount of nickel in the legume family, but still enough that I eat them only in moderation.

Chocolate

Sorry to break it to you, but chocolate boasts a very high nickel content. To get your "chocolate fix" try substituting carob for chocolate in desserts, snacks, and drinks. Carob has moderate amounts of nickel, so can be enjoyed occasionally.

Leafy Greens

I love leafy greens! But kale, chard, spinach, collards, arugula and beet greens contain moderately high amounts of nickel. They have so many health benefits that I still try to include a small amount in my diet. Lettuce contains the lowest amount of nickel among leafy greens.

Other High Nickel Vegetables

Some vegetables are very high in nickel and should be avoided. These include asparagus, okra, sweet potato, fennel, taro root, cassava, and pumpkin. Other vegetables that have moderately high amounts of nickel are parsnips, potatoes, broccoli, artichoke, winter squash, and avocado (technically a fruit).

High Nickel Fruits

Most fruits are fine, but those with high amounts of nickel are raspberries, blackberries, rosehips, pineapple, dates, prunes, figs, pomegranate, persimmon, apricots, plums, passion fruit, star fruit, lychee, and avocado.

Grains, Nuts and Seeds

All nuts and seeds are high in nickel. This is a shame, as they are packed with protein and beneficial nutrients. Be sure to read ingredient listings carefully to avoid nut and seed oils and flours. Oats, quinoa, rice, buckwheat, millet, and amaranth are all high in nickel.

157

Soaps and Cleaning Products

To reduce skin reactions to allergens I use soaps and cleaning products with as few ingredients as possible. I avoid scents, coconut, citrus and citrus based surfactants. My dermatologist recommended Grandma's Pure and Natural brand bar soap for body, and non-detergent laundry soap for clothing. These have been very helpful.

Hair Care

Keeping my hair clean and tangle free was a challenge at first, until I revisited some old time techniques. This is the process I use in place of commercial shampoo and conditioner:

Oil and Vinegar Hair Rinse

Pure Olive Oil
Pure Lye Soap
8 oz. water
2 Tbs cider vinegar

1. Wet hair thoroughly. Place 1/2 tsp olive oil in one hand, and rub hands together. Work oil into hair. Repeat as needed until you have a very light coating of oil throughout your hair. Let sit for a few minutes. *(Be careful not to get oil on the shower floor to avoid slipping.)*

2. Wash hair with a pure lye bar soap such as Grandma's Pure and Natural bar soap. Rinse well.

3. In a squeeze bottle mix 8 oz. of water with 2 Tbs cider vinegar. Apply a small amount to washed hair. Work in for a few minutes then rinse well.

Skin Care

I have not had good luck relying on products listed as hypoallergenic. They can contain coconut, herbal, and citrus products that cause my skin to react. If you are looking for a skin moisturizer consider a simple blend of beeswax and olive oil.

Sometimes I am able to find this at our local farmers market, or you can make your own. It is fairly solid, but the heat from my hands allows me to spread it. Always patch test with a small amount before using.

Beeswax and Olive Oil Salve

1 cup olive oil
2 oz. pure beeswax

Place olive oil and beeswax in a heatproof lided glass jar. Place jar in a sauce pan with enough water to come half way up the sides of the jar. Bring water to a low simmer and stir the olive oil mixture until the beeswax is completely dissolved. Remove from heat and let cool completely before using. Cover and store at room temperature. Can be used as hand and body moisturizer as well as lip balm.

CREDITS & *Acknoledgements*

This cookbook would never have been produced without the encouragement from my family. I'm grateful for my husband, Frederick's patience while food was photographed before getting to the table, and my son Ben's constant requests for recipes. To my mother, Diane, and father Andrew, who instilled in me a love of food. You not only brought me to the finest restaurants, you taught me how to grow and prepare the fruits of our labors. To my Grandmother, Helen, you have passed on to me two of my most valuable gifts, common sense and a fearless ability to adapt. And to my Noni, Ester, you gave me the courage to travel, and to taste and experience the world's diverse flavors. My life is mapped with a joyous assortment of food memories thanks to all of you!

I can't thank our local farmers enough for keeping us healthy and safely away from the grocery stores when the pandemic began. They quickly refocused their marketing from restaurants to local consumers, creating online ordering resources, and contactless pick up. They even supplied spring seedlings for our vegetable gardens.

A special thank you to Skinny Dip Farm, Little Compton RI, Round the Bend Farm and Brix Bounty Farm, Dartmouth MA, Ivory Silo Farm and Weatherlow Farm, Westport MA. I'll never forget the restaurant sized chateaubrion we enjoyed.

I never realized how important recipe testers were until I organized weekly zoom meetings with some of my favorite homeschooled teens. They cooked along side me, and teased out the problems with instructions, and ingredient listings. It was such a pleasure to cook with all of them, and this had the added benefit of keeping us connected once we were no longer able to meet in person. Thank you to Elizabeth Meyers, Lila Goodchild, Ethan, Avery and Aubrey Morgan. You guys rock!

I am grateful to Eva Sommaripa of Eva's Garden for initiating me into the local foraging lifestyle, introducing me to chef and cookbook author, Didi Emmons, and for openning up my eyes to wild foods. Thank you to Didi for putting up with my attrocious spelling, and reviewing a proof of the cookbook. I also want to thank my wonderful editor, Hilly van Loon. Your insights and feedback were invaluable, and your encouragement helped me reach the finish line.

Many years ago we started a wine tasting group with some of our foody friends. We would pick a region or wine type and each bring a bottle and a food from that region. This also led us to olive oil tastings, honey tastings, and salt tastings. I am grateful to Bette Low, Ed Rooney, Kathleen Douley, Roger Cadman, Barbara Smith, Ed Dietric, Joan Menard and Michael Balukonis for sharing their love of food and wine with us and being excellent dessert guinea pigs.

ABOUT *the Author*

Amy Thurber is a multidisciplinary artist and local food enthusiast. After attending Rhode Island School of Design, she produced marketing and packaging design for local farmers and agricultural organizations such as the Coastal Growers Association, NOFA RI, and SEMAP. She was the first farm coordinator for Sharing the Harvest at the Darmouth YMCA, which grows food for distribution through the New Bedford Hunger Commision. While on the board of the Dartmouth Natural Resources Trust she helped start Helfand Farm Community Gardens.

Amy's love of food has grown over the years. It began with the joys of helping her mother make apple pie and bread, and picking peas in her father's large vegetable garden. Her Italian grandmother introduced her to delectible pastries, traditional mozzarella di bufala, and broccoli rabe. She has always had a garden, even when it was just a collection of herbs in pots that traveled with her throughout New Zealand. She continues to share her love of wild and locally grown foods with her homeschooled students through her class *Farm, Forage, Fire*, which culminates with a feast of foraged and locally sourced foods, cooked over an open fire.

When she struggled to change her family's eating habits due to her son's diagnosis of Crohn's disease, and her own numerous allergies, she fully embraced the concept of diet for healing and health. As a decendant of an Abenaki, the Paleo diet appealed to her, as did the concept of healing the gut through the Specific Carbohydrate Diet. Over the past 5 years, Amy has developed recipes to restore her families health, while continuing to bring joy and pleasure through cooking with home grown and local ingredients.

Many of the bowls, leaf plates and platters shown in the recipe photos are examples of Amy's ceramic work. She has always been facinated by pottery and nature, and Doves Foot Pottery has allowed her to explore both for over 15 years. For more information about her ceramics go to https://DovesFootPottery.com.

Amy Thurber is the illustrator and publisher of *In the Wake of the Willows*, by her husband, Frederick Gorham Thurber. *What DO You Eat?* is her first cookbook.

General Index

Winter Savory 79
 Braised Beef Short Ribs 79

Yogurt 18, 85, 100, 129, 139
 Crepes 139
 Pumpkin Pie 100
 Smoothies 129

Zucchini 50, 69, 85
 Minestrone Soup 50
 Zucchini Fritters 69

Wishing You Joyful Eating

—*Amy*

SCD Recipes

Mango Salsa 144
Minestrone Soup 50

N

Navy Bean Hummus 146

P

Pasta & Bean Salad 54
Pea Green Salad 57
Pizza Crust 148
Pork Sausages 37
Port Tenderloin with Dill Sauce 88
Portobello Mushrooms 72
Pumpkin Pie 100
Pumpkin Spice Muffins 33
Pumpkin & White Bean Soup 45

Q

Quiche 91

R

Red Cabbage with Apples 63
Roasted Acorn Squash 74
Roasted Butternut Squash 68
Roasted Carrots & Beets 65
Roasted Dandelion Root Tea 125
Roasted Tomatoes 67
Rose Petal & Lavender Tea 127
Rum-Raisin Cinnamon Bread 29

S

Scrambled Eggs with Herb Butter 35
Simple Pastry Cream 141
Split Pea Soup 46
Sponge Cake 140
Sunflower & Raspberry Linzer Bars

T

Tarragon Chicken Salad 53
Tomato & Turkey Paprikash 90
Turkey Stuffed with Sage 87

W

White Bean Chili 85
White Bean Rosemary Mash 80

Z

Zucchini Fritters 69

PALEO RECIPES

Hold the Cheese Omelet 28
Home-made Garlic Mayonnaise 136
Honey Mustard Marinade 147

Lavender Lemon Balm-ade 127
Lemon Balm Shortbread 111
Lemon Balm Tea 125

Mango Carrot Smoothie 129
Mango Muffins 31
Mango Salsa 144
Mediterranean Tuna Salad 56
Minestrone Soup 50

Navy Bean Hummus 146

Pasta & Bean Salad 54
Pea Green Salad 57
Pesto Mayonnaise 136
Pizza Crust 148
Pork Sausages 37
Pork Tenderloin with Dill Sauce 88
Portobello Mushrooms 72
Pumpkin Spice Muffins 33
Pumpkin Pie 100
Pumpkin & White Bean Soup 45

Quiche 91

Red Cabbage with Apples 63

Roasted Acorn Squash 74
Roasted Butternut Squash 68
Roasted Carrots & Beets 65
Roasted Dandelion Root Tea 125
Rose Petal & Lavender Tea 127
Rosemary-Flax Crackers 120
Rum-Raisin Cinnamon Bread 29

Savory White Sauce 152
Scrambled Eggs with Herb Butter 35
Simple Chocolate Cake 108
Simple Pastry Cream 141
Split Pea Soup 46
Sponge Cake 140
Sunflower Apricot Bars 110
Sunflower Meal 150
Sunflower & Raspberry Linzer Bars
Sweet Potato Puree 70

Tarragon Chicken Salad 53
Toasted Sunflower Seeds 149
Tomato & Turkey Paprikash 90
Turkey Stuffed with Sage 87

Venison Oven Roast 93

White Bean Rosemary Mash 80

Zucchini Fritters 69

Made in the USA
Middletown, DE
03 April 2023

28069332R00102